THE SECRET OF GETTING STRAIGHT A'S

THE SECRET OF GETTING STRAIGHT A'S

Learn More in Less Time With Little Effort

by
Brian Marshall

Illustrations by Bill Ferguson

Hathaway International Publications
P.O. Box 6543
Buena Park, CA 90622-6543

First printing 1993
Second printing 1994

ISBN 0-9633357-9-0

LCCN 92-72740

ATTENTION SCHOOLS, COLLEGES, AND PROFES-SIONAL ORGANIZATIONS: Quantity discounts are available on bulk purchases of this book for educational purposes or fund raising. Special books or book excerpts can also be created to fit specific needs. For information, please contact Hathaway International Publications, P.O. Box 6543, Buena Park, California 90622-6543, or call (714) 772-0109.

To my very special friend
Laura

Acknowledgments

I would like to thank the following people for encouraging me to bring you this book: My parents (Russell and Josephine Marshall) and sisters (Sally Gedney, Kathy Marshall, and Betty Van Malsen), Gina Darnell, Jean Gonzalez, Jeff Bennett, Rolly Collette, Chris Dolas, Lulu Lopez, Dean and Mary Christian, David Shaw, Bill and Marie Ferguson, Dianne Vega, Ross Hirsch, Wayne and Kerrie Woodard, John Duerner, Steve Boers, Gary and Claudia Thompson, Bill Ger, Janet Beisser, Cynthia LaMotte, Scott Kroesen, Bob and Maria Hirsch, Mary McMullin, Larry and Rhonda Clement, Alan and Trena Markus, Betty Barba, Dave Chartier, Joe Barnes, Hyman Crippen, Linda Heiser, Yvonne Walker, Daniel Kaz, David Van Malsen, Bill Gedney, Jameson Garrett, Mary Baumgartner, Scott Buyan, Tony Aldemir, Michael McDonald, Rick Hughes, Paul Hawthorne, Gary Ash, Ed and Cheryl Arismendi, Mark Thompson, Nate Brooks, Ken Cureton, Roger Dawson, Harvey Mackey, Jeffrey Lant, Tom and Marilyn Ross, and the Hall family (Anna, Bert, Judith, Eveline, Theresia, Laura, Darrell, Carrol, and Joanne).

Table of Contents

Preface

Getting straight A's is a symbol of achievement—a source of pride—a mark of excellence. For many it has proven to be an open invitation to the best colleges and highest paying jobs.

Unfortunately, most students aren't taught how to study. They're never shown exactly what to do to achieve high grades. It's for these students that this text has been written.

This book is the result of twenty-five years of research into the easiest and quickest methods for learning and getting top grades. I am not a genius and I've never done very well on intelligence tests. Nevertheless, I am an A student. I discovered at an early age the secret of getting straight A's.

When I was eight years old, I saw my friends and classmates struggling to make good marks. I, on the other hand, breezed through my classes using a simple method for learning and getting top grades. It's helped me maintain an A average throughout grade school, junior high, high school, college, and graduate school.

I've used these techniques to get top honors in virtually every type of class. In addition, I've helped friends and classmates do the same. The formula is fail-proof and works for all subjects including math, science, history, art, foreign languages, and music.

This volume reveals the secret of getting straight A's. Within these pages, you'll find everything you need to know to be a success in school and in life. You'll discover a system that works like magic. And like magic, it's easy . . . when you know the secret.

I have written this book for you. I'd like you to have more of the things you want in life. I hope you want more than you have right now. Because if you do, you have what it takes to be a success. You are ready to use the secrets described in this book.

Introduction

WHO IS THIS BOOK FOR?

It's for anyone who wants a simple formula for success. Are you a top student? Do you breeze through exams with confidence? Is memory your strong point? Do you feel good about yourself and your future? If you hesitate to answer "Yes" to any of these questions, this book is for you.

WHO CAN GET STRAIGHT A'S?

You can! Anyone who applies the information in the following pages can get high grades. You don't have to be a genius. You don't have to "love" school. And you don't have to be the most popular student in class. All you need to do is follow a few simple instructions.

WHY WOULD I WANT STRAIGHT A'S?

You may need them to win a scholarship. You may want them for the knowledge you receive or the success they represent. Or maybe you want good grades to land a high-paying job, increase your self-confidence or gain entrance to a choice college.

Whatever your motivation, the habits you develop as a top student will serve you all your life. These skills make it easy to learn everything you need to know to be a success.

HOW DO I KNOW THE SYSTEM WORKS?

Each technique presented in this book has been tried and tested during the past twenty-five years. The methods have proved effective in virtually every type of class. However, the only way to know the system works is to use it for yourself. Only then will you experience the results. Only then will you realize how easy it is to study, learn, and get straight A's!

1

Construct Valuable Notes

"Taking good notes is like having the answers to test questions before you take your tests."

Getting top grades is really quite easy when you have a system. The best system lets you know what to do every inch of the way. That's exactly what this book provides. Each chapter gives step by step instructions guaranteed to produce results. Your task is to use the information to make your life easier.

Unfortunately, many students make school harder than it needs to be. They see education as a chore and spend their time confused, unmotivated and afraid. In reality, school is very simple. It's made up of only two parts:

1. What you do inside the classroom.
2. What you do outside the classroom.

This chapter covers part one.

Whenever you come to class, there are just a couple things to keep in mind:

1. Follow your teacher's instructions.
2. Take notes.

That's all there is to it.

WHAT ARE NOTES?

Notes are brief writings that point out everything you need to learn to get top grades. They come in two varieties:

1. Furnished Notes

These are hand-outs given to you during class. Ordinarily, they outline your homework assignments, test schedules and the material planned for each class meeting. If you should need them, they'll be supplied by your teachers.

2. Handwritten Notes

Typically, these records are the most important. They're written by you, in your handwriting, and summarize the course material mentioned during class.

WHY WOULD I WANT TO TAKE HANDWRITTEN NOTES?

Well-written notes are your ticket to easy A's. The reason for this is simple: Everything you need to learn to get outstanding grades will be presented or referred to by your teachers during class. This includes the details discussed during lectures as well as any comments about homework and class assignments.

As you listen to and write down this information, your memory retention increases as much as seventy-five percent. Moreover, when you capture these details on paper, you have a simple checklist for getting top grades.

Taking good notes is like having the answers to test questions before you take your tests. These records tell you exactly what to study. And unlike listening to a lecture, you can quickly refer to your notes time and time again.

Taking good notes is like having the answers to test questions before you take your tests.

HOW SHOULD I CONSTRUCT MY HANDWRITTEN NOTES?

1. Bring Needed Tools
2. Sit in the Front Row
3. Listen Carefully
4. Organize Your Notes in Logical Order
5. Include Details
6. Write Legibly
7. Ask Questions
8. Be on Guard for Test Questions
9. Attend Every Class

Bring Needed Tools

It's easy to create outstanding records when you have the proper supplies. The goal is to be well-prepared when you enter the classroom. You can't afford to waste time sharpening pencils or searching for equipment while your teacher is talking.

Therefore, carry a good supply of writing instruments, erasers, and note paper. In addition, you may need to bring textbooks, rulers, etc. It's easy to construct valuable notes when you bring needed tools and sit in the front row.

It's easy to construct valuable notes
when you bring needed tools and
sit in the front row.

Sit in the Front Row

If you're free to choose your place in the classroom, arrive early and take a seat as close to your teacher as possible. The aim is to position yourself where you can see and hear everything presented during class. This is the material you need to learn to be a top student. And it's much easier to capture these details when you sit in the front row. Moreover, you won't be disturbed by noisy students when you take your place at the head of the class.

Here's another reason to sit in the front row: Your teachers will see you and remember you. They'll also notice you if you speak up during class discussions. You'll be amazed at how often this extra visibility will improve your final grade.

Listen Carefully

To create exceptional notes, you need to pay attention to your teacher. Lean forward and hang on every word. Get your body physically involved. By doing this, you'll stay alert and easily jot down the course material certain to earn you top grades.

Organize Your Notes in Logical Order

Teachers make every effort to present information in a sequence you can understand. As a result, it's easy to organize your notes.

Get a notebook and document your first class meeting on the first few pages. Notes from your second session should immediately follow, and so on. Thus, when it's time to prepare for exams, you'll have an organized booklet of notes presented in logical order.

Include Details

When taking notes, write down as much information as possible. Each idea introduced by your teacher could reveal the answer to one or more test questions. Therefore, document all key points including diagrams, charts, and tables. Don't worry about writing too much. Chapter 5 will show you how to recall every detail.

Still, you may be wondering if you can write as fast as your teacher can talk. The answer is: Probably not. But you can keep up with the key points.

For example, suppose your instructor says, "A small pencil is more valuable than a large memory." You may choose to shorten this sentence by writing the following: sml pencil mor val lrg memory. After class, you can re-read your notes and fill in the missing words and letters. But whatever you do, use key words and phrases to capture the main ideas.

Write Legibly

The first rule of good note-taking is this: Write so you can read and understand what you've written. The goal is to avoid spending your valuable time rewriting your notes outside the classroom. However, rewrite them if you feel it will help you to understand better what you've written.

Ask Questions

If you don't understand the material presented during class, ask questions. In most cases your teacher will be your best source of information. Even so, you may be able to find answers in your textbook or library. Or maybe a friend can help.

The important thing to remember is this: Continue asking questions until you understand everything you're required to learn. Then, make a note of this information in your notebook.

Be on Guard for Test Questions

Whenever your teacher speaks, be alert for possible test questions. If you pay attention, you can probably identify material certain to be on your next exam.

For example, at the end of class your teacher may casually say, "Oh, by the way, read page 52 of your textbook before we meet again." Place a checkmark next to these statements in your notebook. These marks will direct your attention to the material most likely to be on your upcoming test.

Oh, and by the way, don't be surprised if you're quizzed on the material presented on page 52 during your next meeting.

Attend Every Class

The only way to be sure your notes are complete is to attend every session from start to finish. The reason for this is that teachers provide clues to test questions at various times during their lectures. Moreover, many educators make important announcements at the beginning and end of class.

As you can see, attending every session is very important. This is especially true on the first day of class. During this gathering, teachers often reveal exactly what you need to do to get top grades. You may receive a course outline, homework and test schedules, and so on. In addition, you may discover how you'll be tested and the factors which determine your final grade.

Attending every class from start to finish is the only way to be sure your notes are complete.

There is yet another reason to aim for perfect attendance: Each class provides a foundation for future learning and makes it easier to understand the material presented in future sessions. If you miss a meeting, you may fall behind in your work and never recover. You can easily avoid this hardship by attending all classes and taking learning one step at a time.

In summary, keep the following in mind whenever you're taking notes: All course material mentioned by your instructors during class is fair game for your next exam.

Each statement could possibly reveal the answer to one or more test questions.

As you become more familiar with your teachers, you'll be able to determine exactly what to write down. Meanwhile, strive to get the overall meaning of the lectures and capture as many key words and phrases as possible. The goal is to create notes which trigger your memory on important ideas discussed in the classroom.

WHAT SHOULD I DO IF I MISS A CLASS?

If an emergency arises, talk with your teacher to find out what was covered while you were gone. Perhaps you can make a photocopy of their lecture material. In addition, get a copy of the appropriate notes from one or two of your brightest classmates. While these records are a poor substitute for attending class, they're the best source of information discussed during your absence.

CONSTRUCTING VALUABLE NOTES— A PERSONAL EXPERIENCE

About twelve years ago I enrolled in a class called Material Joining. During each session, the instructor taught a variety of methods for sticking metals together.

As you can imagine, every student was fighting to stay awake. My only hope for survival was to keep excellent records. I sat near the teacher, leaned forward, and wrote down as many details as possible. My goal was to capture all key ideas mentioned during class.

Five weeks later we had our first test. On the night before, I studied my notes for about three hours. I used them as a checklist. I examined each page to make certain I understood and could apply the information they contained. In addition, I employed the simple memory techniques described in Chapter 5.

As it turned out, the exam dealt with many of the details found in my handwritten notes. I knew the answer to nearly every question and breezed through the test with almost no effort at all. As a result, I received a 93 while the next highest score was only 69.

This story illustrates an important point: Class notes provide a checklist for getting outstanding grades. All you need to do is learn the material outlined in your notebook and your success is almost guaranteed.

Quiz 1

1. School can be divided into two parts: 1. What you do _____ the classroom and 2. What you do _____ the classroom.

2. There are just two things to keep in mind inside the classroom: 1. Follow your teacher's _____ and 2. Take _____.

3. _____ are brief writings that point out everything you need to learn to get top grades.

4. Typically, the most important notes are written in your _____ and summarize the _____ material mentioned during class.

5. Everything you need to learn to receive outstanding grades will be _____ or _____ to by your teachers during class.

6. As you listen to and write down information, your memory retention increases as much as _____ percent.

7. When you keep good records, you have a simple _____ for getting top grades.

8. Taking good notes is like having the _____ to test questions before you take your tests.

9. Unlike listening to a lecture, you can quickly refer to your _____ time and time again.

10. It's easy to create outstanding records when you have the proper _____.

11. If you're free to choose your place in the classroom, arrive early and sit in the _____ row.

12. Sitting in the _____ row will bring you to the attention of your teachers and often improve your final _____.

13. To stay alert while taking notes, lean forward and get your _____ physically involved.

14. Each idea introduced by your teacher could possibly reveal the _____ to one or more test questions.

15. Key _____ and _____ will trigger your memory to recall important ideas mentioned during class.

16. The first rule of good note-taking is: Write so you can _____ and _____ what you've written.

17. If you don't understand the material presented during class, ask _____.

18. Whenever your teacher speaks, be on guard for possible _____ questions.

19. The only way to be sure your records are complete is to attend every class from _____ to _____.

20. On the _____ day of class, teachers often reveal exactly what you need to do to get top grades.

21. School is much easier when you _____ all sessions and take _____ one step at a time.

22. When your _____ are complete, they refer to everything you need to learn to get top grades.

Answers to Quiz 1

1. inside, outside
2. instructions, notes
3. Notes
4. handwriting, course
5. presented, referred
6. seventy-five
7. checklist
8. answers
9. notes
10. supplies
11. front
12. front, grade
13. body
14. answer
15. words, phrases
16. read, understand
17. questions
18. test
19. start, finish
20. first
21. attend, learning
22. notes

2

Tackle Your Homework

*"Touch your homework timidly and it will cut you.
But grab it boldly and you will feel no pain."*

You now know how to spend your time inside the classroom. In the next two chapters, you'll learn exactly what to do outside of it. These chapters provide step by step instructions for completing your homework.

WHAT IS HOMEWORK?

All class activities performed outside the classroom are called homework (term papers, reading assignments, word problems, etc.).

WHY DO INSTRUCTORS ASSIGN THESE TASKS?

Contrary to popular belief, teachers don't give out homework to torture you. They assign it to help you learn more about the subject you're studying.

DO I NEED TO DO ALL OF IT?

Yes. Completing all of your outside assignments is often essential to getting top grades. The reason for this is that homework gives you a chance to practice the material found on tests. Moreover, many educators stamp a point value on all assignments. Each of these scores will be used to determine your final grade.

HOW SHOULD I COMPLETE MY WORK?

Follow these three easy steps:

Step 1: Understand What's Required of You

Before you begin a task, find out exactly what's being asked of you. Typically, you'll be given a written or verbal explanation during class. Therefore, you should have a handy record in your notebook.

*Touch your homework timidly and it will cut you...
but grab it boldly and you will feel no pain.*

Step 2: Start as Soon as Practical

Once you have a clear understanding of your homework, plunge into it as soon as possible. This is a very important step. Getting started is half the battle. When you begin your tasks right away, they become a source of pleasure rather than a source of grief. It's like the old saying: Touch your homework timidly and it will cut you. But grab it boldly and you will feel no pain.

Step 3: Finish What You Start

Rest assured, you'll always complete your assignments when you begin as soon as possible and finish what you start. This doesn't mean you have to do everything all at once. You can usually break big tasks into smaller easy ones. By doing this, you'll be amazed at how fast you can finish your work.

WHAT SHOULD I DO IF I HAVE QUESTIONS?

If you don't understand how to perform a task, find out how to do it right away. Speak to your instructor or locate a tutor outside of class. Or perhaps your notes or textbook can help.

The important thing to remember is this: There are no excuses for unfinished homework. Do whatever is necessary to understand and personally perform all your work. You may need to show knowledge of this material on exams.

WHAT SHOULD I DO IF I'M GIVEN A WRITING ASSIGNMENT?

Follow these five simple steps:

Step 1: Choose a Topic

If you have a choice, select a subject that's clearly defined (that is, a single battle in the American Civil War, a particular current event, and so on). It's much easier to create an essay when you have a specific topic on which to write.

Step 2: Study Your Topic

Learn as much as possible about the theme of your paper. Take extensive notes and/or make photocopies as you do your research. In doing so, you'll be qualified to write on the subject you've chosen. In addition, you'll be able to identify key ideas to include in your work.

1. Choose a topic
2. Study your topic
3. Create an outline
4. Write your paper
5. Read your paper out loud

It's much easier to complete large assignments when you break them into small manageable tasks.

Step 3: Create an Outline

After studying your subject, put together a skeleton. In other words, construct the very first sentence of your paper. Then, list all key points which you feel will make your writing complete. Keep in mind that the first sentence should summarize the overall theme of your essay. Furthermore, each key point should build on this theme and make a good subject for a paragraph.

Step 4: Write Your Paper

Once you've created an outline, it's easy to write your paper. You can begin by constructing the first paragraph and working your way to the end. Or, if you prefer, you can jump around from one paragraph to the other. The important thing to remember is this: Each paragraph should address only one idea.

You may find it helpful to think of each paragraph as a pyramid with a wide base. The first sentence provides a good foundation. The following statements build upon the first. And the last sentence brings the paragraph to a logical conclusion or main point.

Lastly, write a final section that summarizes the overall message of your essay.

Step 5: Read Your Paper Out Loud

The final step is to recite your paper out loud from beginning to end. As you read, you'll probably stumble over some of the words, sentences and paragraphs. These stumbling points usually indicate you need to re-write the material to smooth out the rough spots. Make any necessary changes until you can easily recite your work from start to finish. At that point, you'll have produced a quality piece of writing.

WHAT SHOULD I DO IF
I NEED TO GIVE AN ORAL REPORT?

Once you've mastered the preceding writing technique, it's easy to give oral reports. The procedure is basically the same:

1. Write your paper
2. Practice reading it out loud in front of a mirror
3. Present the report to your class

Don't worry, it's not necessary to memorize your speech word for word. Actually, it's better if you don't. Simply list the key points of your presentation on 3 x 5 index cards. These "cheat-sheets" will trigger important ideas while you're giving your talk. Thus, you'll be relaxed and natural in front of your class. As an added strategy, place a 3 x 5 card on the backside of any prop used in your presentation. This is a beautiful technique. Your audience will see your visual aid and you will see an outline of your speech. What could be easier?

WHAT SHOULD I DO IF I'M OFFERED AN EXTRA CREDIT ASSIGNMENT?

Whenever you're given a chance to boost your final score, take it. Extra credit gives you this opportunity. These assignments are valuable in many ways. First, they show you have a passion for high grades. This extra effort will often convince teachers to give you A's even if you fall short of the required number of points.

Furthermore, extra credit makes you stand out when compared with other students. Frequently, this extra visibility will place you high enough above your classmates to receive outstanding grades.

WHAT SHOULD I DO IF I DON'T HAVE ENOUGH TIME TO COMPLETE MY ASSIGNMENTS?

If you're long on homework and short on time, you may want to use one or more of the following shortcuts:

Read Cliffs Notes
Cliffs Notes are booklets which summarize more than two hundred of the world's great books. They're often found at local bookstores and public libraries. In some

cases you can improve your test scores and cut down your reading time by studying them.

Listen to Books on Tape

If your time is limited, you may be able to complete your assignments by getting books on tape from a local record store, bookstore or public library. These tapes are professionally-produced audiocassette programs containing information found in many popular books.

You may listen to them while driving your car, making your lunch, dusting your room, or just about anything! Often, these tapes will help you finish your reading while engaging in normal daily activities.

Perform Specific Assignments

As a final strategy, spend your limited time doing only those tasks on which you expect to be tested. Obviously, this is more of an art than a science. However, as you get to know your teachers and pay attention during class, you'll gain insight into the material most likely to appear on exams.

DO THESE "SHORTCUTS" ALWAYS PRODUCE DESIRED RESULTS?

No. And here's why: Many teachers want to make sure you do all your work. They often ask test questions concerning the details of your assignments. In these cases, the extent to which you complete your homework can mean the difference between receiving an A and not receiving an A.

WHAT CAN I DO TO GUARANTEE HIGH GRADES ON HOMEWORK?

There are just a couple things to keep in mind:

Complete Your Assignments on Time

It's essential to hand in your work when it's due. Why? Outside assignments provide a base for future learning and make it easier to understand the material presented in future

classes. Conversely, if you delay these tasks, you may
experience the pain of falling behind in your work. Also,
it's bothersome for teachers to correct late assignments and
you're likely to receive lower grades.

Doing all your homework leads to high grades.

Produce Attractive Work

To guarantee high marks, you need to create picture-
perfect products. Neat, accurate, timely work is the trade-
mark of an excellent student. Even if your assignments
aren't completely correct, you'll often receive high scores
simply because they're well-groomed and easy to read.

HOMEWORK MAKES THE DIFFERENCE— A PERSONAL EXPERIENCE

About ten years ago I enrolled in a course called Engineering Economics. I often came to this class with my assignments only partially complete. However, I had an excuse: The teacher didn't present enough information during his lectures to enable me to complete my work. In addition, I felt that studying the textbook was too much trouble. Consequently, I received a C on several exams and decided to drop the class.

I re-enrolled in this course about a year later because it was required for graduation. But this time I looked to myself for responsibility. No blaming and no excuses.

I attended every session with my homework thoroughly prepared. To accomplish this, I often found it necessary to study the textbook and consult the teacher before class. As a result, I received an A on every test and didn't have to take the final exam.

This story illustrates an important point: It's much easier to get top scores when you do your homework. These assignments often make the difference in your final grade.

Quiz 2

1. Homework consists of all class activities performed _____ the classroom.
2. Teachers assign homework to help you _____ more about the subject you're studying.
3. Completing all of your _____ assignments is often essential to getting top grades.
4. Before you begin a task, you need to _____ what's required of you.
5. When you take immediate action on homework assignments, they become a source of _____ rather than a source of _____.
6. An excellent method for completing large assignments is to break them into _____ manageable tasks.
7. There are _____ excuses for unfinished homework.
8. It's easy to produce quality writing when you: 1. _____ a topic, 2. _____ your topic, 3. Create a/an _____, 4. _____ your paper and 5. Read your paper _____ _____.
9. The three steps for giving an oral report are: 1. _____ your paper, 2. Practice reading it out loud in front of a/an _____ and 3. _____ the report to your class.
10. Whenever you're given a chance to boost your final _____, take it.

11. If you're long on homework and short on time, you may want to: 1. _____ Cliffs Notes, 2. Listen to _____ on tape or 3. Perform specific _____.

12. If you delay doing your outside assignments, you may experience the _____ of falling behind in your classes.

13. The extent to which you _____ your outside work can mean the difference between receiving an A and not receiving an A.

14. To guarantee high grades on homework, you need to produce _____, _____, and _____ work.

Answers to Quiz 2

1. outside
2. learn
3. outside (or homework)
4. understand
5. pleasure, pain (or grief)
6. smaller
7. no
8. Choose, Study, outline, Write, out loud
9. Write, mirror, Present
10. score (or grade)
11. Read, books, assignments
12. pain
13. complete (or finish)
14. neat, accurate, timely

3

Optimize Your Study Time

*"Time is your most valuable possession.
Success depends on how you use it."*

In the preceding chapter, you discovered the importance of doing your homework. Each of these assignments can have a big impact on your final grade. Still, you need to develop habits which motivate you to complete your work. But how? The answer is simple: Optimize your study time.

WHAT IS STUDY TIME?

It's the period you invest in homework assignments and preparing for exams.

WHAT'S THE KEY TO WORKING EFFICIENTLY?

If you want to finish your assignments as quickly as possible and still get high grades, you must first picture yourself using your time to best advantage. The reason for this is that your self-image (the way you see yourself) is directly linked to the way you manage your time.

For example, if you see yourself as a goof-off, you'll spend your time goofing off. On the other hand, if you see yourself as an A student, you'll spend a reasonable period hitting your books. Thus, if you want to get top grades with the least amount of effort, you need to fill your brain with the proper mental images.

The next step is to act. That is, you need to get your body physically involved by beginning each task as soon as possible. The following two steps will help you do just that:

Step 1: Create a Motion Picture in Your Mind

Step 2: Act Out Your Motion Picture

The key to working efficiently is to picture yourself using your time wisely and then act out your motion picture.

STEP 1: CREATE A MOTION PICTURE IN YOUR MIND

Before plunging full-steam into your studies, it's wise to develop a plan of attack. Fix in your mind a clear mental picture of the work that needs to be done and your plan for completing it.

For example, imagine it's 3:00 P.M. on Monday afternoon and you have three assignments due on Wednesday at 8:00 A.M. List these jobs on a piece of paper and create a motion picture in your mind.

Imagine yourself going to the library on Monday night. See yourself performing and completing assignment one, two and three. In addition, picture yourself enjoying the process. This one-minute exercise will prepare your mind for the course of action to be carried out that evening.

For the preceding drill to be effective, you must create mental pictures jam-packed with details. That is, you need to see yourself working on specific tasks at a definite time and place. Therefore, the following study tips should be included in your mental rehearsals. These guidelines will help you visualize exactly what to do every step of the way.

1. Make a List
2. Choose a Primary Study Spot
3. Set Aside Enough Time
4. Study by Yourself
5. Keep Your Desk Free From Clutter
6. Take Frequent Breaks
7. Avoid Eating
8. Spend Your Reading Time Wisely
9. Use School to Make Your Life Easier
10. Focus on Rewards

Make a List

Just as a military commander develops a plan of attack, it's a good idea for you to have one also. You can create this plan by listing your assignments on a piece of paper. This outline will provide a roadmap for you to follow. Moreover, you'll enjoy checking each item off the list once it's been completed.

Of course, you'll want to group your work in the order of its importance. However, there may be times when each of your assignments is of equal value. If this should happen, you'll need to know how to organize your work. The following guidelines will help you make the right decisions:

Tackle Unpleasant Tasks First

An excellent method for using time wisely is to perform your least-favorite assignments first. In doing so, you'll complete them without delay and have more time left over for leisure. Conversely, if you postpone these tasks, they may become a source of anxiety and frustration. And you may be tempted to put them off indefinitely. You can't allow this to happen if you want to get top grades.

Avoid Studying Similar Subjects

To get the most from your study time, don't study subjects such as algebra and trigonometry in a given time-frame. These topics can be a source of confusion and your mind may jumble one with the other. Therefore, leave a half-hour or so in between. You can usually fill this gap by learning different material or simply taking a break.

Choose a Primary Study Spot

A terrific way to condition yourself to study is to set up a primary learning place. Ideally, it should include a desk and a chair. The chair should support your lower back and allow you to sit up straight. Learning can be tiring and a chair that supports your lower back helps prevent premature fatigue.

This area should also contain adequate lighting that illuminates your work place, but does not reflect light into your eyes. This type of lighting will keep your eyes from tiring and allow you to study for a longer time.

As a final thought, your main study spot should be free from outside disturbances such as TV, telephones, music, and voices. Learning requires concentration and it's much easier to concentrate when you can hear yourself think. Also, you won't be tempted to abandon your work when you go to a secluded area.

Still, if you must listen to songs while studying, listen to slow mood music rather than lively pop or rock music. The rhythm and beat of slow melodies is more conducive to learning.

Set Aside Enough Time

To complete your assignments successfully, you need to allow sufficient time to complete your work. For example, when writing a term paper, you may want to set aside two hours three days a week for four weeks. You'll probably want to work at the same time and place each day. That way, you'll condition yourself to study. You'll associate this time and place with learning new information.

Certainly this approach is more realistic than expecting to complete your paper in a single evening.

Study by Yourself

As a rule, you learn faster and better when you study alone. Studying is not a social activity. It often requires deep thought and concentration. Furthermore, it's easy to dawdle and waste time in the presence of others. Thus, if you want to complete your assignments in the shortest time, find a quiet place to call your own.

Keep Your Desk Free from Clutter

You'll find that it's much easier to concentrate when you keep a clean and tidy work area. The reason for this is simple: If you have books and papers scattered on your desk, your mind will tend to wander. You may find yourself reaching for papers and picking up books which have nothing to do with the subject on which you're working.

In short, you drain your energy and reduce your effectiveness when your work place is untidy and disordered. So, if you want to increase the fruits of your study time, work on one task at a time and keep your desk free from clutter.

You'll finish your assignments quicker when you work on one task at a time and keep a clean and tidy work area.

Take Frequent Breaks

If you find yourself getting bored or tired while studying, take a break. It's amazing how refreshing a short recess can be. At times, all you need to do is sit at your desk and stretch as if you were yawning. At other times, you may want to walk around for a couple of minutes or take a leisurely stroll to the drinking fountain.

Take these breaks quietly and by yourself every fifteen to thirty minutes. The goal is to rest before you get tired. These brief intermissions will recharge your batteries and allow you to relax, sort and store the information. As a result, you'll reduce the amount of time you would otherwise spend studying.

Avoid Eating

You may feel like snacking while you're learning new material. However, it's best to stay away from refreshments. You don't burn many calories while studying and eating is an unnecessary distraction that interferes with your concentration.

Moreover, your energy goes to digest the food and your brain slows down. You can't afford to have this happen if you desire good grades. You may want to use food as a reward for completing your work, but avoid eating during your learning time.

Spend Your Reading Time Wisely

Reading assignments can consume a tremendous amount of time. Thus, you'll want to do everything possible to use your time to best advantage.

Keep in mind that comprehension is more important than speed. Read at whatever pace is comfortable for you and follow the three steps presented below:

Step 1: Warm Up

Step 2: Read Straight Through

Step 3: Look For Likely Test Questions

Step 1: Warm Up

Just as a boxer warms up before a fight, it's a good idea to warm up before you read. The goal is to get a general background on the material you're about to study.

For example, if you're going to read the first three chapters of a book, begin by scanning the material on the front and back covers. Then, read the short biography of the author located on the inside jacket of many books. This quick and easy overview lets you know who wrote the book and why.

As you read, use one of your fingers to underline and point to the words on the page. This technique helps you learn at whatever pace you desire. In addition, you'll find that it's easier to concentrate when you get your body physically involved.

Next, look at the table of contents and introduction. This material gives further insights into the book you're about to study. You'll also find it helpful to browse through the pages and make mental notes of information presented in bold face type, italics, tables, charts, and summary paragraphs.

Lastly, if there are questions at the end of the chapters, read them before you begin. This approach will help you recognize important ideas when you see them.

Step 2: Read Straight Through

After warming up, run through each chapter in its entirety. Don't stop to ponder details not immediately clear as you read. Rather, plow through each page like a story-book and strive to follow the author's main ideas.

Ideally, this step should be completed before going to class.

Step 3: Look For Likely Exam Questions

Sometime after class, go through each assignment again. But this time, make up test questions as you read. Focus on the key ideas presented in each chapter (that is, material discussed during class, answers to questions found at the end of chapters, and so on). This is what your teacher will do when putting together an exam.

Use a highlighting pen (or pencil-in a checkmark) to mark the information you expect on your upcoming test. Continue in this manner until you've finished reading each assignment a second time.

At this point, you may be wondering if you need to take notes while reading. The answer is: No. You can usually read the highlighted sections perhaps five or six times in the time it takes to write the same material only once. However, there is an exception to this rule.

Take notes only if you anticipate test questions on material not specifically mentioned in your text. For example, if you're taking a history class, you could expect to be asked to list historical events in the order in which they occurred. Yet, this information may not be spelled out in your book.

Therefore, flip through the pages and record each event and the date it took place. Then, list them in chronological order in the margins of your textbook or in your handwritten notes. This technique provides a complete picture of important details and makes it easier to prepare for exams.

While reading your assignments, take notes if you feel it will help you remember better what you've studied.

The three steps presented above will help you learn the information in your reading assignments. You'll find that it's easy to grasp the full meaning of all significant points in the shortest amount of time. In addition, the highlighted passages provide a neat and convenient way to get ready for tests.

Still, if you're like most people, all this reading may seem like a lot of work. Don't worry. You probably won't always need to read your assignments a second time. In fact, in some classes you won't need to read them at all.

The reason for this is that outside reading is often used to restate some of the key points mentioned during class.

However, in many cases these assignments also include additional information considered outdated and unimportant by teachers.

In these instances, very few test questions (if any) will come from your textbooks. As a result, you'll waste a lot of time if you always follow the three steps described above.

Therefore, you may choose to use the three-step procedure when priming yourself for the first exam in each of your classes. This approach will ensure that you're well prepared.

After taking the first test, you'll know if you need to continue reading your assignments. After all, your instructors will probably test you the same way in the future. Armed with this information, you'll be able to determine how much time (if any) you need to invest in future reading.

Use School to Make Your Life Easier

Whenever possible, use what you learn in class to enhance your life. For example, suppose you're learning multiplication. You can use this knowledge in a grocery store. It's often necessary to multiply one number by another to arrive at a total price. Thus, you can practice what you learn and reinforce your education. As a result, you'll make your life easier and remember the material for a longer time.

Focus on Rewards

Finally, if you want to motivate yourself to study, focus on the rewards of completing your work. Think about the many reasons why getting good grades is important to you (scholarships, high-paying jobs, increased knowledge, etc.). In addition, direct your attention towards any treats you can give yourself when you finish your assignments. These thoughts will help you avoid the pain and misery that comes from falling behind in your work.

STEP 2: ACT OUT YOUR MOTION PICTURE

Once you've created an emotionally-charged detailed motion picture, put it into action at the specific time you've set. As you continue to act, you'll discover an amazing phenomenon. You'll find that you feel good about yourself and your ability to get things done. You'll also be motivated to continue pushing forward until you've finished all your work.

Still, there may be times when you lack energy to complete your assignments. On these occasions you may want to take a nap. If that's not possible, eat a piece of fruit to raise your blood sugar level. In addition, walk around to get your blood flowing. Finally, take several deep breaths to help you think more clearly. These steps will boost your energy and allow you to complete your assignments on time.

As a final note, there may be occasions when you feel fed up with studying. If this should happen (and time permits), treat yourself to a movie, a restaurant, or one of your favorite activities. Have as much fun as you possibly can.

By studying before you have fun, you'll finish your tasks sooner and have something to look forward to while completing your work.

When you're done, be sure to complete your work. The goal is to associate studying with having a good time. As a result, you'll complete your assignments and enjoy the process of going to school.

Be warned, however! Don't let the above strategy become a habit. You'll enjoy learning much more when you study before you have fun. In doing so, you'll finish your tasks sooner and have something to look forward to while completing your work.

IS THERE ANYTHING ELSE
I SHOULD KNOW ABOUT STUDYING?

Yes. You can create new and fun ways to enjoy your study time. For example, you may want to record your class lectures or dictate your class notes into a tape recorder. You can listen to these recordings while doing the dishes, making your bed, or driving your car.

The above technique is not intended to replace the study habits discussed thus far. However, you may want to use your imagination to make learning more enjoyable and make the best use of your time.

MAKING THE MOST OF STUDY TIME—
A PERSONAL EXPERIENCE

Several years ago I needed to write a term paper for an English course. During class, the teacher described the assignment. He told me to go to the library and gather some facts on gun control. Then, I was to write a paper on what I'd learned.

What a boring assignment, I thought. I had six weeks to complete it and no enthusiasm to start it. However, as I looked around the room, I noticed all the other students had the same attitude. Everyone thought the assignment was a waste of time.

At that point, I decided to take control of my thinking. I developed a plan of attack by picturing myself going to the library at 11:00 A.M. that very day. I was determined to spend an hour and a half gathering facts on gun control. Then I took action!

I went to the library Monday, Wednesday, Friday and all day Saturday for the next two weeks. The librarian helped me find everything I needed. As a result, I completed the assignment one month ahead of time.

However, the best part was yet to come: I had a tremendous amount of leisure during the next four weeks, and received an A on my paper. Moreover, I escaped the grief and agony that many of the other students experienced when their essays came due.

This illustrates an important point: It's easy to complete your assignments when you plan your work and work your plan. By doing this, you finish your tasks in record time and have time left over for leisure.

Quiz 3

1. Study time is the period you invest in _____ assignments and preparing for _____.
2. Before plunging full-steam into your studies, it's wise to develop a/an _____ of attack.
3. An excellent method for developing a plan of action is to _____ your assignments on a piece of paper.
4. If you want to use your time wisely, tackle unpleasant tasks _____.
5. To avoid confusion, don't study _____ subjects back to back.
6. A good way to condition yourself to study is to set up a/an _____ study spot.
7. To complete your assignments successfully, set aside enough _____ to complete your work.
8. To develop good habits, strive to study at the same _____ and _____ each time you study.
9. As a rule, you learn faster and better when you study by _____.
10. It's much easier to concentrate when you keep your _____ free from clutter.
11. To increase your retention of study material, take frequent _____.
12. You may want to use food as a reward for completing your work, but avoid _____ while studying.

13. Outside reading is often used to _____ some of the
    _____ _____ mentioned during class.

14. Reading assignments often include information that's
    considered _____ and _____ by teachers.

15. When reading your assignments, _____ is more
    important than speed.

16. It's a good idea to _____ _____ before reading.

17. After warming up, _____ each chapter without
    stopping and strive to follow the author's _____
    ideas.

18. To improve your concentration and speed while
    reading, use one of your _____ to underline and
    point to the words on the page.

19. Highlighted reading passages provide a neat and
    convenient way to prepare for _____.

20. When performing reading assignments, take _____
    if you feel it will help you to remember better what
    you've studied.

21. By using what you learn in school, you _____ the
    material for a longer time.

22. To motivate yourself to study, focus on the _____
    of completing your work.

23. It's easy to complete your assignments when you
    _____ your work and work your _____.

Answers to Quiz 3

1. homework, exams
2. plan
3. list
4. first
5. similar
6. primary
7. time
8. time, place
9. yourself
10. desk
11. breaks
12. eating
13. restate, key points
14. outdated, unimportant
15. comprehension
16. warm up
17. read, main
18. fingers
19. exams (or tests)
20. notes
21. remember
22. rewards
23. plan, plan

Prepare to Conquer Exams

*"It's not the smartest student who gets A's on tests,
it's the student who's best prepared."*

At this point, it should be clear how to spend your time inside and outside the classroom. All you need to do is take notes and follow your teachers' instructions while inside, and complete your assignments outside. These habits really pay off when it's time to prepare for exams.

WHAT ARE EXAMS?

They're tests used to determine how well you've mastered your course material. They are often written by instructors and contain questions about lectures and homework assignments.

WHY DO I NEED TO PREPARE FOR EXAMS?

Your final grade is often based on how well you take tests. Thus it pays to exercise great care in getting ready. Remember, it's not the smartest student who gets A's on exams, it's the student who's best prepared.

It's not the smartest student who gets A's on tests,
It's the student who's best prepared.

WHEN SHOULD I START GETTING READY?

If you've attended all your classes and kept up with your homework, you can usually start preparing a day or two ahead of time. The goal is to give yourself enough time to review your study material two to five times before the test. As you become more experienced, you'll be able to determine exactly how much time this will take.

WHAT MATERIAL SHOULD I COVER?

Your class notes point out everything you need to study. Invariably, they'll refer to one or more of the following:

Lecture Material

Homework Problems

Reading Assignments

Past Exams

The Upcoming Test

Just as a pilot uses a checklist to fly an airplane, class notes provide you with a checklist when preparing for exams.

Lecture Material

The best source of study material is usually the lecture material found in your handwritten notes. This information is favored by your teachers and is most likely to appear on exams. After all, instructors often know the test questions in advance and design their lectures accordingly. Therefore, it's wise to spend most of your time learning this information.

Homework Problems

Ideally, you should review all problems found in your outside assignments. You need to be happy with your ability to solve each one. You'll probably have to tackle similar questions on exams.

Reading Assignments

As a rule, you don't need to re-read your textbooks. Simply study the highlighted passages and any notes you may have taken. This is the material you expect on your upcoming test and you'll want to spend a portion of your time reviewing it.

Past Exams

Old tests, given to classes in years gone by, are an excellent source of study material. They often contain the same questions found on current exams. If they're available, be sure to include them in your study plan.

The Upcoming Test

During class, many educators give clues as to the questions you can expect on exams. This is especially true during the class just before a test. As a result, you'll want to spend some time learning this material.

Even so, it's a good idea to ask instructors what you should study. If possible, find out the number and types of questions (true/false, multiple choice, etc.). This information will help you develop a sound plan of attack.

In addition, you may be able to talk with your teachers' former students. They can often help pinpoint the kinds of questions you're certain to come across. If you're lucky, they may even have past exams available for review.

HOW SHOULD I GO ABOUT
STUDYING THIS INFORMATION?

The following six-step learning process makes it easy to prepare for exams:

Step 1: Assemble Study Material

Step 2: Read the First Section

Step 3: Hide the First Section

Step 4: Recite the First Section

Step 5: Study the Remaining Sections

Step 6: Review Each Section

Step 1: Assemble Study Material

First, gather your test material (class notes, homework problems, reading assignments and previous exams). Look it over to get an idea of what you need to do. Then, divide the information into logical sections.

Step 2: Read the First Section

Examine the first part carefully. Study this material as if you needed to teach it to someone else. Then, make up possible test questions and commit your answers to memory. This is the most important part of preparing for exams.

Step 3: Hide the First Section

Place what you've just read where you won't be able to see it.

Step 4: Recite the First Section

Recite what you've just studied (out loud if possible) while creating clear mental pictures in your mind. In doing so, you'll remember the information better and determine exactly what you've learned.

Step 5: Study the Remaining Sections

Repeat steps 2, 3 and 4 for each of the remaining sections.

Step 6: Review Each Section

Lastly, go over each segment at least one more time to be sure you've learned the material. In many cases, you'll need to cover each section three to five times before you've mastered it.

As a final strategy, give yourself a practice test at the end of your study session. Use the questions you created in Step 2. If possible, write your answers on a piece of paper while reciting the information out loud.

The above exercise will dramatically increase your retention and boost your confidence on the day of your test. After all, you probably will have studied the answers to most questions you'll find on the actual exam.

*To boost your self-confidence before an exam,
give yourself a practice test.*

IS THERE ANYTHING ELSE I SHOULD KNOW ABOUT PREPARING FOR TESTS?

Yes. Whenever possible, use the following guidelines:

Sleep Soundly

The best thing to do, if you want to remember what you've learned, is to go to sleep when you finish studying. This allows the information to set in your brain.

Be careful however! Take a few minutes to unwind before retiring. Otherwise, you may toss and turn all night long. Perhaps you can watch a comedy, listen to some soothing music, or drink a glass of milk. By doing this, you'll find that it's much easier to fall asleep and retain what you've studied.

Test Yourself Upon Waking

Once you've come back to life, give yourself a quiz. This technique will reinforce what you've learned and reveal any areas on which you still need to work. You can test yourself while taking a shower, making your bed, or driving your car. If you're unsure of an answer, simply refer to your notes.

CONQUERING EXAMS— A PERSONAL EXPERIENCE

About sixteen years ago, I enrolled in a class called Physical Anthropology. During the semester, I wrote a term paper, learned the names of 125 human bones, and studied the evolution of the human species. Nevertheless, my final grade was based on how well I performed on the final exam.

One week before the end of the semester, the instructor told the class exactly what to study. We were urged to review specific lecture material, handouts, and reading assignments. But most importantly, we learned that many of the final exams, given in years gone by, were available in the school library.

As far as I know, I was the only student to study the old tests. I went to the library and hand-wrote the questions and answers to more than one hundred multiple choice questions. I studied this material using the six-step study system until I could recite it in my sleep.

To my joy and amazement, roughly seventy percent of the final exam consisted of questions from the previous tests. As a result, I earned an easy ninety percent. The next highest score among my classmates was somewhere in the low eighties. Consequently, I was the only student to receive an A on the final and the only one to get an A in the class.

This illustrates an important point: You can achieve outstanding scores when you use the six-step study system and anticipate the test questions. You don't have to be a genius. All you need to do is be prepared.

Quiz 4

1. _____ are used to determine how well you've mastered your course material.
2. Exams are often written by _____ and contain questions about _____ and _____ assignments.
3. Your final grade is often based on how well you take _____.
4. Typically, you need to get ready for exams a/an _____ or two ahead of time.
5. The best source of study material is usually the _____ material found in your handwritten notes.
6. You should be able to solve all problems contained in your _____ assignments on the day of your tests.
7. When preparing for tests, study the _____ sections of your reading assignments and any _____ you may have taken.
8. Old _____, given to classes in years gone by, are an excellent source of study material.
9. Before studying for an exam, ask your instructor what material you should _____, and the _____ and _____ of questions you can expect.
10. To learn at a deep level, study as if you needed to _____ the material to someone else.

11. The most important part of preparing for exams is to anticipate _____ questions and commit your answers to _____.

12. You may need to review each section of your study material _____ to _____ times before you've mastered it.

13. It's a good idea to give yourself a practice _____ at the end of your study session.

14. The best thing to do, if you want to remember what you've learned, is to go to _____ when you finish studying.

15. Upon _____, test yourself to see how well you retained what you studied.

16. It's not the smartest student who receives A's on exams, it's the student who's best _____.

Answers to Quiz 4

1. Tests (or Exams)
2. instructors, lectures, homework
3. tests
4. day
5. lecture
6. homework
7. highlighted, notes
8. exams
9. study, number, types
10. teach
11. test, memory
12. two, five
13. test
14. sleep
15. waking
16. prepared

5

Unleash Your Super Memory

*"The more ways your brain senses something,
the better it remembers it."*

In the preceding chapter, you discovered how easy it is to prepare for exams when you use the six-step study system. In addition, you were asked to anticipate the test questions and commit your answers to memory. But how can you remember all this information? The answer is simple: Unleash your super memory.

HOW DOES MY MEMORY WORK?

Generally speaking, your memory works by linking each of your experiences with a mental picture or pictures. These images are the language of your subconscious mind. You dream in pictures and you think in pictures. And whether you realize it or not, many of the thoughts that flash through your mind have mental cartoons associated with them.

For example, do you see a pink elephant in front of you at this very moment? Actually, this is a trick question. To answer it, you must first imagine what a pink elephant looks like. Your mind then quickly compares your mental picture with the image it actually sees.

This is typical of how your memory works. It simply links each of your thoughts with a mental picture or pictures.

HOW CAN I DEVELOP A SUPER MEMORY?

The key to a powerful memory lies in your ability to link one thought (or mental picture) with another. This is a natural way to think and you do it all the time.

For instance, you connect one thought with another whenever you have a conversation. Your words trigger thoughts in the minds of the people with whom you talk. Likewise, their words trigger thoughts in your mind. As a result, your dialogue goes back and forth. One thought is linked with another.

*The key to a super memory lies in your ability
to link one thought with another.*

This linking process is the key to a super memory. All you need to do is hook your thoughts together until you remember what you want to recall.

For example, suppose you want to remember to take out the garbage tomorrow morning. Place a waste basket at the exiting doorway of your house. Tomorrow morning, as you're about to leave, you'll see the trash can. This image will cause you to remember to unload the rubbish. Thus, one thought (mental picture) triggers another until you recall the desired information.

HOW CAN I USE MENTAL PICTURES TO HELP ME REMEMBER THINGS?

All you need to do is associate a mental image with the details you want to learn. This brain cartoon will then trigger your memory to recall specific facts.

For instance, suppose you want to commit to memory the definition of the word jovial. Jovial means "full of playful good humor." You can remember this definition by slicing the word into pieces and linking a mental picture with one or more of the parts. In this case, you may want to cut it in two: jo vial.

Close your eyes and picture a fifty-foot man named Jo playing with a ten-foot vial full of laughing gas. He's tossing it in the air and catching it in his mouth. Imagine that Jo is full of playful good humor as he breathes the gas from the vial.

Now, whenever you see the word jovial, you'll think of Jo and the vial full of laughing gas. With a little practice, you'll associate this ridiculous mental picture with the proper meaning of the word.

Brain cartoons can also help you become an exceptional speller. For example, suppose you want to remember how to spell believe. Slice the word into small pieces and link a mental picture with each part. In this instance, you may want to cut it into three sections: Be li eve (pronounced "be lie eve").

Next, close your eyes and imagine a twenty-foot bee telling a lie during the evening. It has a round body, swollen lips, and a long nose like Pinocchio. Now, whenever you want to remember how to spell believe, you'll be reminded of the bee telling a lie during the evening. With a bit of practice, you'll link this ridiculous mental picture with the proper spelling of the word.

It's much easier to remember two or more small words than to remember one large one.

You can use mental pictures to help you remember almost anything. Simply break the information into sections and associate a mental picture with one or more of the parts. Then, whenever you want to remember specific facts, one thought will trigger another until you think of the information you desire.

IS THERE SUCH A THING AS A "RIGHT" OR "WRONG" MENTAL PICTURE?

No. However, there is such a thing as a *good* mental picture. It's any image that causes you to remember what you want to recall. An effective way of creating these pictures is to make them ridiculous, colorful, larger than life and moving—animate them.

There's a direct relationship between your senses and your memory. The more ways your brain senses something, the better it remembers it. Therefore, you need to create images which force your brain to sense information in a variety of ways.

An easy way to accomplish this is to first, establish what you want to remember. Then, slice the information into sections and link a mental picture with one or more of the parts. Finally, test yourself to see if your images trigger the proper response.

If they do, great! If not, make your pictures larger, more colorful, more ridiculous and/or filled with more action. These brain cartoons will logically lead you to the desired information.

HOW CAN I REMEMBER ALL THE DETAILS IN MY NOTES?

The secret to remembering a vast amount of data is really quite simple. All you need to do is commit to memory a list of key words. Key words are terms which trigger thoughts in your mind and help you remember huge amounts of information.

For example, what do you think about when you hear the word "birthday"? Chances are, you can recall many of your past birthdays and many of the parties you've attended. The key word (birthday) triggers your memory to retrieve a tremendous number of details.

Likewise, you can find key terms in your notes which cause you to remember all the information they contain. For instance, suppose you want to commit to memory the nine guidelines for taking notes presented in Chapter 1:

1. Bring Needed Tools
2. Sit in the Front Row
3. Listen Carefully
4. Organize Your Notes in Logical Order

5. Include Details
6. Write Legibly
7. Ask Questions
8. Be on Guard for Test Questions
9. Attend Every Class

Choose one word from each guideline which you feel will trigger your memory to recall the entire guideline. Then, print them on a piece of paper. In this case you could write the following key words:

1. Tools
2. Sit
3. Listen
4. Logical
5. Details
6. Write
7. Ask
8. Guard
9. Attend

Next, write down the first letter of each term: T S L L D W A G A. Now, rearrange these letters to form a word (or words). In this instance, you could create STLLD WAGA (pronounced "stalled waga"). Then, whenever you want to recall the nine guidelines for taking notes, simply think of STLLD WAGA.

With a little practice, you'll associate the S with Sit, the T with Tools, the first L with Listen, the second L with Logical, the D with Details, the W with Write, the first A with Ask, the G with Guard and the second A with Attend.

These nine key words will cause you to remember the nine guidelines for taking notes. Moreover, once you've thought of them, you'll recall at least one paragraph of information about each.

At this point, you may be wondering whether you'll be able to recall the memory aid STLLD WAGA. If so, close your eyes and picture a nine-ton poodle sitting on your class notes. Imagine the poodle has a stalled automobile engine inside its rear end. This broken down motor is keeping the poodle from wagging its tail. In other words, the dog has a STLLD WAGA.

In a short time, you'll be able to recall this ridiculous mental picture whenever you need to list the nine guidelines for taking notes. And like a chain reaction, you'll remember the nine key words and all the information associated with them.

The above technique makes it easy to remember a list of key words and, hence, all the details in your notes. Moreover, if your records are complete, you'll probably commit to memory nearly all the answers to questions you'll find on exams.

ARE THERE OTHER WAYS TO USE KEY WORDS?

Yes. You can use them to help you prepare for multiple choice tests when you have access to past exams. For example, suppose you're studying the following multiple choice question:

The main trait which determines a student's success in school is the student's:

A) Past achievements

B) Level of motivation

C) Age

D) Level of income

Suppose B is supplied as the correct answer. Simply locate a term in answer B that doesn't appear in the other choices. In this instance, "motivation" is a logical key term because it's only found in choice B.

Now, make a connection between "motivation" and a key word (or words) found in the first part of the question. In this case, "main" and "trait" are logical key terms. Therefore, create a link between "main trait" and "motivation."

You can accomplish this by making up a rhyme such as: "The main trait is motivate." Repeat this verse several times out loud while picturing yourself as a motivated student. This technique will logically lead you to the correct answer should you find the above question on an exam.

*Key words can lead you logically
to the correct answers on tests.*

HOW CAN I MEMORIZE SPECIFIC FACTS?

When you need to learn information word for word, simply recite it over and over to the same rhythm and beat. For instance, consider the following meaning of success:

The progressive realization of a desired goal.

Recite this definition again and again to the same rhythm and tempo. Perhaps you can record your voice using a tape recorder. Then, listen to the recording in a relaxed environment while reading the words out loud. Read, recite and listen and you'll memorize information at an amazingly rapid rate. The words become absorbed in your mind much like the lyrics to a song or the alphabet you learned as a child.

If you need to memorize a longer passage, read it over and over in the manner described above. Once the rhythm and sound of the words become familiar to you, recite the entire message all by yourself. If you forget the words, glance at the text to refresh your memory.

Continue reciting the material until you have it memorized. Then, repeat the words now and then throughout your day. This type of spaced repetition will etch the message deep into your subconscious mind. Eventually, you'll be able to recite the entire passage with almost no effort at all.

ARE THERE OTHER MEMORY TRICKS I SHOULD KNOW ABOUT?

Yes. At times, you may want to use one or more of the following techniques to help you remember numbers:

Rhyming Verses

Rhymes are an excellent way to help you remember important facts. For example, you may recall the following: *In fourteen hundred and ninety-two (1492) Columbus sailed the ocean blue*. This rhyme associates the explorer with the year he discovered America. As a result, it's easy to remember 1492. Likewise, you can create your own rhyming verses to help you recall important historical dates.

Rhythm and Beat

Another memory trick is to recite numbers out loud to your own creative rhythm and beat. Simply repeat them over and over to the same tempo. You probably learned your phone number in a similar manner and can recite it with very little effort. You simply start at the beginning and the rest of it flows naturally.

Number Games

You can also remember numbers by playing games with them. For example, consider the following quantity: 62,348,224. It's awkward to think of this figure as sixty-two million three hundred forty-eight thousand two hundred twenty-four. Therefore, you may want to cut it into pieces and play a game with each part.

In this case, you can break it in two: 623 and 48224. Now, think of each section as the final score of a sporting event: 6 to 3 and 48 to 24. This is just another way of saying 6 two 3 and 48 two 24 (or 6 2 3 and 48 2 24). As you can see, it's much easier to remember two or more small numbers than it is to remember a very large one.

Getting top grades is easy when you commit to memory the answers to test questions before you take your tests.

You now have a series of techniques to help you remember numbers, memorize facts, and recall important details in your notes. These methods will help you file information neatly in your mind and have it readily available for recall on the day of your tests. If you use them conscientiously, you'll commit to memory nearly all the answers to test questions before you take your tests.

MEMORY MAKES THE DIFFERENCE— A PERSONAL EXPERIENCE

About two and a half years ago, I enrolled in a four-week course called Expert Systems. I attended every class, took extensive notes and performed all assignments. As a result, I received an A on the midterm and an A on the class project. Still, the last exam determined my final grade.

On the night before the test, I studied my notes for nearly four hours with a half-hour break after the first two hours. I anticipated the questions and committed my answers to memory using the memory tricks described in this chapter. Lastly, I gave myself a practice test and wrote my answers on a piece of paper. By the end of the evening I was confident I would receive an A on the final exam.

The next morning, I took the test and knew the solution to practically every question. It was almost too easy. I'd committed to memory nearly all the answers the night before. As a result, I received an A on the final and an A in the class.

This story illustrates an important point: In many classes you can earn A's simply by anticipating test questions and storing the answers in your mind. In doing so, you'll learn the material better and are likely to know most of the answers before you take your tests.

Quiz 5

1. Generally speaking, your memory works by linking each of your experiences with a mental _____.
2. The key to a super memory lies in your ability to link one _____ (or mental picture) with another.
3. You can create _____ cartoons which trigger your memory to recall almost anything.
4. A good mental picture is any image that causes you to _____ what you want to recall.
5. You can create good mental images by making them _____, _____, _____ than life and in _____.
6. The more ways your brain _____ something, the better it remembers it.
7. The secret to remembering a vast amount of data lies in your ability to remember a list of _____ words.
8. _____ words are terms which trigger thoughts in your mind and help you remember huge amounts of information.
9. To memorize information, recite it over and over to the same _____ and _____.
10. Spaced _____ is the key to long-term memory.
11. It's easy to recall important numbers when you include them in a/an _____.
12. It's much easier to remember two or more _____ numbers than it is to remember a very large one.

13. In many classes you can earn A's simply by antici-
    pating _____ questions and committing your
    answers to _____.

Answers to Quiz 5

1. picture
2. thought
3. brain (or mental)
4. remember
5. ridiculous, colorful, larger, motion
6. senses
7. key
8. Key
9. rhythm, beat
10. repetition
11. rhyme
12. small
13. test, memory

6

Master the Art of Taking Tests

"Often, it's not what you know, but how well you take exams that determines the final grade in your classes."

At this point, you're ready to unlock the final skill which leads to your success in school. You have taken extensive notes, tackled your homework, and stored this information neatly in your mind. You are now ready to master the art of taking tests.

IS TEST-TAKING REALLY AN ART?

Yes. It takes a lot of creativity and strategy to do well on exams. Often, it's not what you know, but how well you take tests, that determines the final grade in your classes.

WHAT KINDS OF TESTS CAN I EXPECT?

Typically, you'll be given one or more of the following:

True/False
Multiple Choice
Matching
Fill-in-the-Blanks
Essay/Oral
Problem-Solving

Each of these tests gives you an opportunity to show how well you prepare for exams. Moreover, each one challenges your strategies for achieving the highest possible score.

True/False

These tests include a series of statements. Your task is to determine which are true and which are false. For example:

Circle T for True and F for False

T F 1. If you want to get outstanding grades, you need to take personal responsibility for the results in each of your classes.

T F 2. A students are always the smartest students in class.

Number 1 is true. If you want to be successful in school, you need to look to yourself for responsibility. You must be willing to put forth the necessary effort to guarantee success.

Number 2 is false. A students are not always the smartest. Often, they simply go to class, take notes, do their homework and study for exams. These activities don't always require a lot of brain power.

As you can see, true/false tests are very simplistic. You read a series of statements and indicate which are true and which are false.

You can often answer test questions by tossing out choices you know are incorrect.

Multiple Choice

These tests include questions which offer several possible answers. Your job is to choose the best response. For example:

Which of the following is/are not part of the six-step study system?

A) Assemble study material
B) Sit in the front row
C) Review each section
D) A and C

The correct answer is B. And here's why: Answers A and C are part of the six-step study system. Therefore, they can be eliminated. In addition, D can be thrown out because it contains A and C. Since B is not part of the six-step study system, it's the best answer.

Multiple choice questions should be read very carefully. In doing so, you'll have a better chance of picking the proper response. Furthermore, you can often arrive at the best answer by tossing out choices you know are incorrect.

Matching

These tests consist of information to be matched-up with related information. For instance:

Match the terms on the left with the appropriate definition on the right.

___ 1. Lecture material

A) Terms which trigger thoughts in your mind and help you remember huge amounts of information.

___ 2. Past exams

B) The details most likely to appear on exams.

___ 3. Key words

C) Questionnaires which often contain the same types of questions found on tests.

In this case, 1. is B, 2. is C, and 3. is A.

Admittedly, matching exams are a lot like true/false and multiple choice tests. In each case, all of the answers are supplied to you (that is, T, F, A, B, C, D, and so on). Your task is to simply choose the best response.

Fill-in-the-Blanks

These tests are found at the end of each chapter in this book. They include statements which have key words missing. For example:

Taking good _____ is like having the answers to _____ questions before you take your tests.

During an exam, you would complete the above statement by writing the words "notes" and "test" where you see the blanks. Your paper would then look like this:

Taking good <u>notes</u> is like having the answers to <u>test</u> questions before you take your tests.

These exams require you to have key words and phrases immediately available for recall on the day of your tests. Thus, it's good practice to commit to memory a lot of details. In doing so, you'll find that fill-in-the-blanks tests are simply a matter of answering questions you addressed while preparing for the exam.

Essay/Oral

These two tests are much the same. They both give you an opportunity to express your ideas freely. The main difference is that essay tests are written and oral tests are spoken. For instance, consider the following essay/oral question:

What material should students study when preparing for exams?

These types of questions can be answered in three parts:

1. Opening Sentence
2. Body
3. Conclusion

Opening Sentence: This is the first statement in your answer and should clearly address the question being asked. You can often create this sentence by rephrasing the exam question. For example, look at the following opening sentence:

Students should study the details mentioned in their class notes when preparing for exams.

As you can see, the sample question was simply reworded. This technique gets you started on the right track.

Body: The body of your answer should build on your opening sentence and can be anywhere from one sentence to many paragraphs in length. For example, you might create the following body:

If these records are complete, they'll refer to all the material on which students will be tested and graded.

This statement builds on the opening sentence. It provides an excellent reason why students should learn the information in their notes.

Conclusion: The last part of your answer should contain one or more statements which bring your response to a logical close. The purpose of this section is to capture the overall theme of your answer. For example, you might compose the following conclusion:

Therefore, it's a good idea to use furnished and handwritten notes as a checklist when getting ready for tests.

The above sentence captures the general thrust of your answer and brings it to a reasonable end. Your entire response would then look like this:

Students should study the details mentioned in their class notes when preparing for exams. If these records are complete, they'll refer to all the material on which students will be tested and graded. Therefore, it's a good idea to use furnished and handwritten notes as a checklist when getting ready for tests.

As you've probably noticed, essay and oral exams give you an opportunity to show how much you know about the subject you're studying. You can easily answer these questions in three parts: 1. Opening Sentence, 2. Body and 3. Conclusion. In other words, 1. Tell them what you're going to tell them, 2. Tell them, and 3. Tell them what you've told them.

Problem-Solving

These tests give you a chance to apply your knowledge. For example:

How long will it take a train traveling 55 miles per hour (mph) to travel 165 miles? (Note: Assume the train will travel at a constant speed of 55 mph during the entire trip).

Questions of this nature test your powers of insight and creativity. This is why you must be able to solve problems contained in your homework, handwritten notes, and reading assignments. Your knowledge of this material makes it easier to answer questions on problem-solving exams.

You've now seen the most popular tests given in school: true/false, multiple choice, matching, fill-in-the-blanks, essay/oral, and problem-solving. Nevertheless, you may still be a little nervous about taking exams. If so, have no fear. Help is on its way.

HOW CAN I AVOID PRE-TEST JITTERS?

It's perfectly normal to be a little nervous before an exam. In fact, it can actually be an advantage. When you're nervous, you're more alert. And if you're prepared, you're likely to respond quickly and accurately to questions.

Still, it's not a good idea to be too restless on the day of a test. It's far better to be confident and self-assured. The following guidelines will help you achieve this positive state of mind:

1. Eat a Healthy Meal

2. Dress Up
3. Bring Needed Supplies
4. Arrive Early
5. Avoid Pre-Test Chatter

Eat a Healthy Meal

To stay strong and energized, eat a healthy meal at least an hour before test time. Include foods such as whole grain breads, cereals, and fruits. They'll feed your mind and body with energy-producing nutrients. As a result, you'll perform better during your exam.

Dress Up

You'll feel more relaxed and comfortable when you dress up on the day of your tests. It's much easier to concentrate when you're not worried about your appearance. When you look good, you feel good. You stand a little taller and think a little quicker. As a result, you're likely to earn better grades.

Bring Needed Tools

To be confident and self-assured, carry all important supplies into the testing room (a wrist watch, plenty of sharp pencils, erasers, books, paper, test booklet, calculator, etc.) These tools will help you focus on the questions and achieve your highest possible score.

Arrive Early

One of the easiest ways to avoid pre-test jitters is to arrive early and relax in the seat of your choice. Find a quiet place where you'll be calm and undisturbed. Keep in mind, however, that instructors often give clues during tests. Therefore, you'll want to position yourself where you can see and hear all instructions given by your teacher.

As you sit quietly before the test, take several deep breaths and imagine yourself answering every question easily and effortlessly. This is a very important step. In doing so, you'll clear your mind and eagerly await the opportunity to show what you've learned. Moreover, you'll avoid the mental confusion experienced by those students who stroll into class moments before the test.

As you sit quietly before a test, take several deep breaths and imagine yourself answering each question easily and effortlessly.

Avoid Pre-Test Chatter

It's quite common to see students testing one another during the hour before an exam. Do not, however, engage in this activity. The reason for this is that random cramming is likely to confuse you and make you anxious. It's much better to check your notes only if you have specific questions. That way you're certain to implant nothing but correct information in your brain.

WHAT GAME PLAN SHOULD I FOLLOW WHEN I RECEIVE MY TEST?

There are seventeen strategies to keep in mind. They'll help you get outstanding scores on all types of exams.

1. Jot Down Notes

After writing your name on your answer sheet, jot down any important notes and/or formulas while they're still fresh in your memory. These notes may help you answer questions later on.

2. Read Instructions

Next, carefully examine the test instructions. You must understand exactly what's required of you. Remember, not all tests are the same and you may find slight differences among them.

3. Examine the Test

Before marking your answer sheet, scan the test to determine what types of questions you need to answer. Be on the look-out for those you can respond to easily and accurately. Keep in mind that you're setting up a plan of attack for achieving the highest possible score.

4. Answer Easy Questions First

Once you're familiar with the test, answer the simple questions first. In doing so, you'll build momentum and increase your confidence.

5. Answer All Questions

Next, answer all remaining questions in numerical sequence. Start from the beginning and work your way to the end. This technique will help you avoid skipping questions accidently.

As you work your way through the exam, answer each question to the best of your ability. If you're unsure of an answer, write down the first hunch that flashes into your mind. Otherwise, make a reasonable guess. That's right, guess! In most cases you're not penalized for guessing and your score can only improve when you guess correctly.

Lastly, make every effort to avoid skipping questions. You may not have time to come back to them. However, if you do jump over problems, place a checkmark next to them so you can quickly return to them later.

As you continue through the exam, your subconscious mind will help you discover solutions to the questions you skip. In some cases the correct answers may even be revealed somewhere in the remainder of the test. With a little luck and proper planning you'll have time to go back and fill in the proper responses.

6. Read Questions Carefully

It's important to examine each question carefully before arriving at an answer. A common mistake is to form an opinion before reading the entire question. You can avoid this blunder by looking over each problem in its entirety before drawing any conclusions.

Furthermore, be alert for qualifying phrases such as "all the following except", "which of the following are not", and so on. In addition, be on the look-out for words such as "always" or "never." These words often indicate a false answer. On the other hand, words such as "usually", "rarely" and "sometimes" often indicate a true response.

Still, there may be times when you don't understand a question. If this should happen, ask your instructor to clarify its meaning. If you're lucky, your teacher may even divulge the correct response while attempting to answer your query. In any event, speak only to the person conducting the exam. Otherwise you may be accused of cheating.

7. Mark Your Answer Sheet Carefully

As you work your way through an exam, exercise great care while filling in your answers. If you jump around from question to question, be certain to mark the appropriate spaces. In doing so, you'll receive maximum credit for each correct response.

8. Budget Your Time

Usually, time is the most important factor to keep in mind while taking tests. You must divide it up properly. For example, if a test is worth 100 points (two questions worth 25 points and another worth 50) spend one-fourth of your time on each 25-pointer and half your time on the one remaining. The objective is to answer all questions to achieve your highest possible score.

Nevertheless, there may be occasions when you run out of time before completing an exam. If this should happen, you can improve your score by jotting down the main points to the remaining questions. Be sure to include an answer for each.

In addition, you may want to write a note to your instructor ("I ran out of time," for example). If your teacher knows you and believes in your sincerity, you may even receive high scores for work only partially complete.

As a final thought, do everything in your power to make each minute count. For instance, if you're taking a matching test, cross out matches so you don't waste time re-reading them a second or third time. This approach will ensure that you use your time wisely to achieve an excellent score.

9. Draw Pictures

Occasionally, you'll find it helpful to make a sketch of the problems you need to solve. Draw your pictures carefully to avoid careless mistakes. These diagrams will help you visualize exactly what to do. As a result, you'll have an easier time arriving at solutions.

10. Show Your Work

Whenever possible, include (on your answer sheet) all the steps you follow in answering each question. This information will help you stay focused on what you're doing. Furthermore, you'll often be graded on the details presented on your paper. Your instructor will look at these steps to assign your final grade. Thus, you'll probably receive a good score even if you make a few mistakes.

11. Don't Second-Guess Your Answers

You'll improve your chances for high grades if you avoid looking at the previous answers on your answer sheet. There's usually no pattern to these responses. If you do see one (A A B B C C, etc.), don't be fooled into making any changes. You'll do much better if you respond to each question based on your knowledge of the subject being taught.

12. Be Creative

In some instances the solution to test questions may not be obvious. This can happen even when you're thoroughly prepared. In these cases you need to exercise your imagination.

Simply relax and reflect on the material you studied while preparing for the exam. Think of the steps involved in your homework assignments and problems presented during class and in your textbook. If you're well-prepared, you'll probably be able to use these ideas to answer even the most troublesome questions. Who knows, you may even come up with a solution that no one has ever thought of before.

13. Take Mini Breaks

Taking tests is a lot like studying. You need to take short breaks now and then to clear your mind. The aim is to rest before you get tired. You'll be surprised at how refreshing a twenty-second recess can be. It gives you a chance to recharge your batteries and helps you perform very well on exams.

14. Write Neatly

To improve your chances for high scores, print your answers carefully. In doing so, you'll be able to read your own writing and are less likely to make careless mistakes.

For example, if you're taking a math test, be sure to copy numbers accurately, align columns and write as neatly as possible. This approach will make your job easier and reduce the number of reckless errors. Moreover, instructors will often reward your neatness with higher grades. Write your answers neatly to avoid careless mistakes and achieve higher scores.

Write your answers neatly to avoid careless mistakes and achieve higher scores.

15. Include Details

If time permits, inject as many relevant facts in your answers as possible. These details reveal how much you know about the subject you're studying. The more correct information you include, the more likely you are to receive maximum credit.

It's also a good idea to answer questions in the same way your teacher presented the material during class. You can't go wrong using the same words as your instructor.

Still, there may be times when you don't know the answer to a particular problem. If this should happen (during an essay exam, for example), write as much correct information as possible in your response. Don't worry if your answer doesn't specifically address the question being asked.

You'll be amazed at the results. Many teachers will award points whenever you display detailed knowledge of the subjects they teach. This is an excellent way to receive credit for questions that leave you completely stumped.

16. Defend Your Reasoning

To improve your chances for high scores, you must be able to defend the reasoning behind each of your responses. In other words, you need to know why your answers are correct. This technique will help you build confidence in your ability to solve problems. Moreover, you may need to protest the answers to questions you miss.

17. Review Your Answers

If you still have time after completing your test, take a few moments to relax and clear your mind. Then, review your paper at least one more time. Start from the beginning and work your way to the end. Re-read the test instructions and check each of your answers.

Never turn in an exam when you still have time to review it. You'll probably find at least one mistake. Remember, it's okay to be the last student to finish. Use every available minute and don't leave until you are convinced that you've done your best.

Finally, don't change an answer unless you're confident in what you're doing. Your first response is more likely to be correct. After all, your first solution is calculated when you're still fresh and alert.

WHAT SHOULD I DO AFTER I HAND IN MY ANSWER SHEET?

Give yourself a special reward as soon as possible. Treat yourself to a movie, a choice restaurant, or one of your favorite activities. The goal is to associate studying and taking tests with having fun. In doing so, you'll look forward to studying for future tests and the good times that are certain to follow.

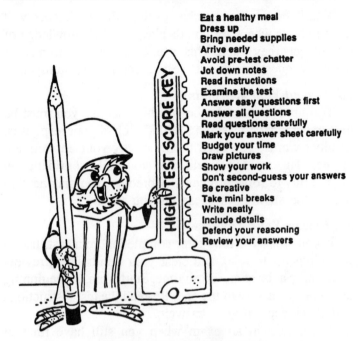

Eat a healthy meal
Dress up
Bring needed supplies
Arrive early
Avoid pre-test chatter
Jot down notes
Read instructions
Examine the test
Answer easy questions first
Answer all questions
Read questions carefully
Mark your answer sheet carefully
Budget your time
Draw pictures
Show your work
Don't second-guess your answers
Be creative
Take mini breaks
Write neatly
Include details
Defend your reasoning
Review your answers

HIGH TEST SCORE KEY

*The key to high test scores
is a strong plan of attack.*

WHAT SHOULD I DO WHEN THE TESTS ARE RETURNED?

First, take a few moments to bask in the glory of your victory. You followed the system and now there's a big, fat, juicy A on your paper. Enjoy the warm feeling of success. It's a feeling you'll want to experience time and time again.

Next, take extensive notes as your teacher reviews the test. Write down everything your instructor says about the exam. This includes all the questions you answered correctly as well as any you may have missed. If no review is given, ask for one during your teacher's office hours.

The reason for this is that questions covered during post-test reviews are often found on future tests. When you capture this information in your notes, you gain insight into the material your instructor feels is important. Moreover, you make it easy to prepare for coming exams.

*To help you do better on future tests,
take extensive notes during post-test reviews.*

WHAT SHOULD I DO IF I
DON'T GET AN A ON A TEST?

The first thing you need to do is maintain a positive mental attitude. Don't compare yourself with other students. Rather, focus your attention on your past successes and remind yourself that you're a winner.

Once you've gotten over the initial shock and controlled your state of mind, there are five courses of action which will help you move closer to your goal of high grades:

1. Check for Errors in Grading
2. Talk with Your Teacher
3. Learn from Your Experiences
4. Vow to Do Better Next Time
5. Drop the Class (if necessary)

Check for Errors in Grading

Whenever you miss a test question, check for blunders made during the grading of your paper. This is an excellent method for improving your score.

In addition, you may need to protest the answers to questions you miss. The reason for this is that some tests are poorly written and may have several correct solutions. As a result, you can often improve your score by showing why your answers are correct.

Talk with Your Teacher

In many classes you can improve your grade by having a chat with your instructor. Most teachers will do everything they can to help you. After all, your progress is directly related to how well they're doing their job. Never accept a low score as final until you've sorted things out with the person in charge of the grades.

Learn from Your Experiences

It's much easier to achieve top grades when you make a habit of gaining from your experiences. For example, if you don't get an A on a test, find out where things went wrong. Maybe you missed a class or misread some of the questions. Whatever the explanation, there's a good chance you can learn from the incident and move closer to reaching your goal.

Vow to Do Better Next Time

If you receive a score that isn't up to your standards, vow to do better next time. Remember, one low grade is not a disaster. You can often develop a new strategy and raise your future scores to soaring heights.

Drop the Class

If an important test score is very low or if a class just isn't working out, you may be able to drop it before a final grade is placed on your permanent record. Don't be afraid to exercise this option. Often, this approach will help you regroup and come back stronger than ever.

STRATEGY: THE KEY TO HIGH TEST SCORES— A PERSONAL EXPERIENCE

About ten years ago, I took the most incredible true/false exam of my life. I came to class early and relaxed in my favorite front row seat. I also cleared my mind by taking several deep breaths and imagining myself answering every question easily and effortlessly. In addition, I ignored the pre-test chatter taking place around me.

When I received the exam, I read the instructions and developed a plan of attack. I then answered each question in numerical order by selecting the first answer that flashed into my mind. In some cases I found it helpful to draw a sketch.

When I finished the test, I reviewed my responses and was confident I could justify each one. Just then I noticed something amazing: All of my answers were marked "True." I'd never seen anything like it before and began to wonder if I'd made a mistake.

I reviewed the exam one more time and was tempted to make some changes. However, a little voice inside my head told me not to. It said, "Your first response is more likely to be correct. Don't change an answer unless you're confident in what you're doing." As a result, I handed in my paper with every answer marked "True."

When the tests were returned, I was the only student to receive a perfect paper. Each of my classmates had been fooled into changing their answers. Consequently, they lowered their scores.

This story illustrates an important point: To get outstanding grades, you need to know how to take tests. Often, it doesn't matter how much you know, it's your strategy that counts.

Quiz 6

1. Tests give you an opportunity to show how well you _____ for exams.
2. You can often arrive at the best _____ by tossing out choices you know are incorrect.
3. When you commit to memory a lot of _____, you'll often find that tests are simply a matter of answering questions you addressed while _____ for the exam.
4. During essay and oral exams, the _____ sentence should clearly address the test question.
5. The body of your answers can be anywhere from one _____ to many _____ in length.
6. The conclusion should contain one or more _____ which bring your response to a logical close.
7. Problem-solving tests often contain questions similar to those found in your _____, _____ notes and _____ assignments.
8. To stay strong and energized on the day of your tests, eat a healthy meal at least a/an _____ before test time.
9. One of the easiest ways to avoid pre-test jitters is to arrive _____ and _____ in the seat of your choice.

10. To improve your chances for high grades on tests, arrive early and imagine yourself answering every question _____ and _____.

11. To avoid confusion, stay clear of _____ cramming and pre-test _____.

12. After writing your name on your answer sheet, jot down any important _____ and/or _____ while they're still fresh in your mind.

13. After jotting down notes, read the _____ carefully.

14. Once you've examined the test, answer the _____ questions first.

15. If you're unsure of an answer, write down the _____ hunch that pops into your mind.

16. If you decide to skip a question, place a/an _____ next to it so you can quickly return to it later.

17. A common mistake is to jump to a conclusion before reading the entire _____.

18. It's a good idea to wear a wrist watch to help you keep track of _____.

19. Typically, you should include a/an _____ for all questions.

20. A/An _____ can help you visualize the solution to some problems.

21. Whenever possible, include (on your answer sheet) all the _____ you follow in answering each question.

22. There's usually no pattern to the _____ on answer sheets.

23. If the solution to a problem is not obvious, simply _____ and reflect on the _____ you studied while preparing for the exam.

24. Taking short _____ will recharge your batteries and help you do well on exams.

25. You'll improve your chances for high scores when you write your answers _____.

26.   The more correct information you include in your answers, the more likely you are to receive _____ credit.

27.   To improve your chances for high scores, you must be able to defend the _____ behind your answers.

28.   If you still have time after completing your test, take a few moments to _____. Then, re-read the test _____ and check each of your responses.

29.   When taking tests, _____ every available minute and don't leave until you're convinced you've done your _____.

30.   Don't change an answer unless you're _____ in what you're doing.

31.   During post-test reviews, take extensive _____.

32.   Whenever you miss a test question, check for _____ made during the grading of your paper.

33.   Never accept a low grade as final until you've talked with your _____.

34.   If an important test score is very low or if a class just isn't working out, you may be able to _____ the class.

Answers to Quiz 6

1. prepare
2. answer
3. details, preparing
4. opening
5. sentence, paragraphs
6. statements
7. homework, handwritten, reading
8. hour
9. early, relax
10. easily, effortlessly
11. random, chatter
12. notes, formulas
13. instructions
14. easy
15. first
16. checkmark
17. question
18. time
19. answer
20. sketch (or picture)
21. steps
22. answers
23. relax, material
24. breaks
25. neatly

26. maximum
27. reasoning
28. relax, instructions
29. use, best
30. confident
31. notes
32. errors
33. teacher
34. drop

7

Discover How You Learn

"By exercising your imagination, you can take what you learn in school and turn it to your advantage."

The system presented in this book is one of the easiest methods ever created for getting outstanding grades. It's so simple, it's almost like baking a cake. When you follow the steps, you'll know the answers to test questions before you take your tests. As a result, you can get high scores in any class—even classes you dislike.

Nevertheless, getting good grades is not the main reason to go to school. Education is intended to increase your knowledge and improve your quality of life. For this reason, you'll often want to thoroughly absorb the material in your classes. This chapter will show you how. You'll discover exactly what to do to completely learn anything you desire.

HOW DO I LEARN?

You learn by experiencing life through one or more of your senses. Whenever you see, hear, taste, smell, touch, "think" or "feel" something, your subconscious mind stores the information. Amazingly, this part of your mind remembers every detail of your life and never forgets anything.

You learn by experiencing life through one or more of your senses.

THEN WHY DO I FORGET THINGS?

This happens because you're not always able to locate the information stored in your subconscious mind. You may "know" it's there, but you just can't find it. This occasionally happens to everyone. But it won't happen to you when you actively participate in the learning process.

HOW CAN I DO THAT?

Follow these five easy steps:

    Step 1: Repeat Your Experiences
    Step 2: Understand Your Experiences
    Step 3: Practice What You've Learned

Step 4: Creatively Use Your Knowledge

Step 5: Re-use Your Knowledge from Time to Time

Step 1: Repeat Your Experiences

One of the easiest ways to learn is to simply repeat your experiences. For example, whenever you see a movie more than once, you retain more of the details. You recall more of the scenes and remember more of the dialogue.

It's easy to recall any event when you relive it again and again. However, this type of learning is often brainless and narrow-minded. You simply put your brain in neutral and recite a bunch of facts. To gain a greater depth of knowledge, you need to do more than that.

Step 2: Understand Your Experiences

This is the foundation of quality learning. When you understand an experience, you give meaning to it. For instance, think back to when you were learning to ride a bicycle. Before your feet ever touched the peddles, you watched other people as they glided like the wind on two wheels. Thus, you understood the purpose of riding bicycles before ever experiencing the thrill yourself.

Once you comprehend and give meaning to something, you're ready to advance to the next step.

Step 3: Practice What You've Learned

If you really want to understand something, you need to use your mind and body to practice what you've learned. You can use your hands, eyes, ears, voice, and mental pictures. In doing so, you'll employ more of your senses. And the more senses you use, the better.

For instance, think back once again to when you were learning to ride a bicycle. You understood "the basics" by observing other people. However, something exciting happened when you gripped the handle bars, perched yourself on the seat and started pumping the peddles. Your mind and body became physically involved. As a result, the experience was deeply implanted in your memory.

To really understand something,
you need to practice it.

Similarly, in school you'll have plenty of chances to practice what you've learned (while doing homework, taking tests, etc.). However, these activities are often mechanical and require very little creative thought. If you want to get the most from your education, you need to use your knowledge to accomplish specific tasks. The following step will help you put this idea into action.

Step 4: Creatively Use Your Knowledge

The best way to learn is to creatively use your education to help you reach your goals. For example, you've discovered that the more ways your brain senses something, the better it remembers it. You can creatively use this knowledge whenever you want to learn the material on audiocassette tapes.

After you've listened to a tape once or twice, listen to it again. But this time, repeat key words and phrases out loud as you hear them. At the same time, imagine you're the expert delivering the message. This technique will bring more of your senses into play. As a result, you'll exercise your creativity and remember the details for a longer time.

The preceding example illustrates an important point: You can use your imagination to create new and better ways of doing things. In fact, Albert Einstein used to say that "Imagination is more important than knowledge." By exercising this faculty of your mind, you can take what you learn in school (or anywhere else for that matter) and turn it to your advantage.

You now have four steps for learning anything you desire. These guidelines will help you start from the beginning, understand the basics, and build upon what you already know. This is the key to carefree learning. Even so, there's one more step you need to know about.

Step 5: Re-use Your Knowledge from Time to Time

Whenever you employ one or more of the preceding four steps, you create a "pathway" in your mind. It leads from your conscious mind to your subconscious mind.

Imagine that this "pathway" is like a trail from your house to your school. Each time you hike on it, you create a clearer path on which to walk. Likewise, each time you repeat a learning experience, you create a clearer "pathway" in your mind.

These tracks will remain clear as long as you practice what you've learned. However, "weeds" can grow on them when you don't use your knowledge for extended periods. Therefore, you must use your education from time to time to maintain clear "pathways" in your mind. This is the only way to be sure you'll remember what you've learned.

*When it comes to knowledge, you can either
use it or lose it.*

As you can see, this fifth and final step is essential to successful learning. To fully grasp a subject, you need to perform all five: 1. Repeat your experiences, 2. Understand your experiences, 3. Practice what you've learned, 4. Creatively use your knowledge, and 5. Re-use your knowledge from time to time.

THE FIVE-STEP LEARNING PROCESS— A PERSONAL EXPERIENCE

About two years ago I completed a Masters degree in software engineering. There were sixteen courses in the program and each one lasted four weeks. That's right! One class per month for sixteen months.

When I entered the program, I had no background in computers. I started from the beginning and steadily built a foundation of knowledge. Each class prepared me for the next. And I took every opportunity to understand and practice what I learned.

As time went by, I creatively applied the teachings in each class. I saw how each subject related to the others. And before every exam, I reviewed my notes to clear the "pathways" in my mind. As a result, I learned the material and graduated with a 3.93 G.P.A.

This story contains all the elements in the five-step learning process. See if you can find them. These steps will help you learn anything you desire. All you need to do is start from the beginning, understand the basics, and build upon what you already know.

Quiz 7

1. One of the easiest ways to learn is to _____ your experiences.
2. When you _____ an experience, you give meaning to it.
3. To improve your level of understanding, you need to use your _____ and _____ to practice what you've learned.
4. The more ways your brain _____ something (hearing, taste, sight, etc.), the better it remembers it.
5. The best way to learn is to creatively _____ your education to help you reach your _____.
6. By exercising your _____, you can take what you learn in school and turn it to your advantage.
7. To remember what you've learned, you need to use your _____ from time to time.
8. You can learn anything when you start from the _____, _____ the basics, and build upon what you already _____.

Answers to Quiz 7

1. repeat
2. understand
3. mind, body
4. senses
5. use, goals
6. imagination (or creativity)
7. knowledge (or education)
8. beginning, understand, know

8

Gain the Winner's Edge

"The one who tries with the most ploys wins."

In the preceding chapter, you learned how to build a storehouse of knowledge. You discovered the five steps for learning anything you desire. Nevertheless, grades are still important. They're a yardstick to measure your progress in school. Moreover, they often open doors leading to the best colleges and highest paying jobs.

If success is your goal, you need to use every available trick. Remember, you'll be compared with other students and you must stand out in a favorable way. The following twelve strategies will help you do just that:

1. Believe in Your Ability to Learn
2. Like Yourself
3. Vow to Be an Excellent Student
4. Look to Yourself for Responsibility
5. Relate Each Class to Your Vision and Purpose
6. Read Your Textbooks Early
7. Take Fun Classes

8. Get to Know Your Teachers
9. Choose Your Friends Carefully
10. Select Inspiring Role Models
11. Aspire to Perfect Health
12. Keep a Sense of Humor

Believe in Your Ability to Learn

To be successful in any undertaking, you must first have faith in yourself. This is certainly true in school. More than ninety percent of your success in learning is due to your belief in your ability to learn.

For example, many people think they're terrible in arithmetic. They tell themselves over and over that math is a tough subject. In addition, they've probably missed some classes and fallen "hopelessly" behind. As a result, they now believe they can't work with numbers.

Even so, most people have plenty of talent for mathematics. All they need to do is tell themselves they're good at it, learn the basics, and build upon what they already know. Given enough time and motivation, these people can learn anything. And so can you! If you believe in your ability to learn, your success is practically guaranteed.

Like Yourself

It's much easier to achieve high grades when you value and respect yourself. The aim is to like yourself regardless of how pretty you are, how much money you have, or the number of A's on your report card. In doing so, you'll make the journey to your goals a sincere pleasure every step of the way.

Vow to Be an Excellent Student

If you want to rise to the top of the class, pledge to be an outstanding student. It's much easier to stay motivated when you're good at what you do. For example, think of an activity at which you're highly skilled. Chances are, you enjoy this pastime and spend some time practicing it.

Similarly, you'll be an excellent student when you make the commitment and invest your time accordingly.

Look to Yourself for Responsibility

To gain the winner's edge, you must take personal responsibility for the results in your classes—no blaming and no excuses. For example, have you ever tried hitting a baseball with a baseball bat? If so, you know that you need to swing the bat in such a manner that it smashes the ball into the field.

However, if you don't make contact, do you blame the bat? The ball? The field? Of course not. You look to yourself for responsibility and adjust your mental attitude, stance and swing. Likewise, if you have a difficult teacher or a class that bores you, look to yourself for solutions and make whatever changes are necessary to guarantee success.

Relate Each Class to Your Vision and Purpose

This step will help you maintain your passion for high grades. All of your courses are important. Each one brings you closer to your goals (scholarship, high-paying job, increased knowledge, etc.). When you keep this in mind, you'll eagerly learn the material in every class.

Read Your Textbooks Early

One of the easiest ways to get a jump on your courses is to read the first two or three chapters of your textbooks before your first class meeting. This approach gives you a head-start and helps you stay current with your work. Not only that, you'll feel terrific about yourself because you lived up to your promise to be an excellent student.

Take Fun Classes

The system presented in this book will help you get top grades in any subject. However, if you want to have more fun, enroll in courses you enjoy. Certainly this is not always possible. But if you have a choice, take classes that interest you most.

Get to Know Your Teachers

One of the best ways to improve your chances for high marks is to get acquainted with your instructors. They're the ones who assign your grades and it pays to know what makes them happy.

In some instances, you can learn about your teachers before you enroll in their classes. You may be able to talk with former students or members of the faculty. These folks can help you decide whether or not to take certain courses.

The important thing to remember is this: If you have a choice, select instructors who love to teach. These educators are eager to help you succeed. Besides, they make even the most difficult subjects fun to learn.

In other instances, you won't have the luxury of choosing your schoolmasters. At times like these you can learn a lot by paying attention during class. This is the material favored by your instructors and may provide clues into what makes them tick.

In addition, you can outshine your classmates by developing friendships with your teachers. Sometime during the beginning of each term, ask what you need to do to get an A in their class. Armed with this information, you're bound to have an advantage. Not only that, you may even receive high grades simply because your instructors like you.

Choose Your Friends Carefully

To improve your chances for outstanding grades, you need to thoughtfully select the company you keep. For example, you may have noticed that drug addicts usually hang around other drug addicts. Conversely, top students often befriend other top students. This is not a coincidence. If you want to rise to the top and fly with the eagles, you can't afford to hang around turkeys.

One of the best ways to improve your chances for high grades is to get to know your teachers.

Select Inspiring Role Models

An excellent way to gain the winner's edge is to watch and imitate successful people. Do what they do and you're certain to enjoy similar results. For instance, think of a person who's accomplished what you want to achieve. If you study them, you'll find you have a lot in common. Moreover, you'll be filled with a sense of possibility: "If they can do it, then I can do it!" In many cases this thought will be all you need to carry you to success.

Aspire to Perfect Health

To enjoy increased energy and a sense of well-being, you need to take care of your health. Regular exercise and proper nutrition do amazing things for mental and physical strength. Exercise produces a natural high and stimulates your body into action. In addition, it's a great way to reduce stress.

Similarly, well-balanced meals provide your body with the fuel it needs to drive you to the top. Furthermore, you can often improve your I.Q. and test scores simply by improving your diet.

Keep a Sense of Humor

Unless you're from another planet, you've probably found that things don't always go your way. You may do everything right and still get a ticket from a local policeman. You may study intently for a math test and yet receive a low test score because you forgot to learn a small detail mentioned at the end of one class.

At times like these, the best thing to do is keep a sense of humor. Create a story in your imagination that makes you laugh at the situation. Winners understand that nothing outside of themselves can control their inner attitude. As a result, you'll never waste time worrying about things you can't change. Instead, you'll experience the joy that comes from taking charge of your thoughts.

The twelve strategies described above will help you stand out when compared with other students. Often, this extra visibility will place you high enough above your classmates to receive outstanding grades.

By standing out in a favorable way,
you're bound to receive outstanding grades.

FRIENDS MAKE THE DIFFERENCE— A PERSONAL EXPERIENCE

About three and a half years ago, I was fed up with working full-time and going to school full-time. I was physically and mentally exhausted. To put it mildly, I had a negative mental attitude and needed a check-up from the neck up!

In an effort to change my negative thinking, I began to listen to inspiring audiocassette programs while driving my car. These excellent recordings were available at a local library and had titles such as *Think And Grow Rich* by Napolean Hill and *The Psychology Of Success* by Brian Tracy.

I was entertained and stimulated by the ideas on these tapes. As a result, I began to focus on my goals and renewed my commitment to complete my education.

Nevertheless, as time went by school became more difficult. I was struggling to survive and didn't think I could handle all the assignments. Consequently, I wanted to drop out of the program. But two of my closest classmates, Tony and Doris, convinced me to hold on for one more class.

The next course was a nightmare! I didn't understand the material and was rapidly falling behind. I was a nervous wreck and wanted to quit. But one thought from *Think And Grow Rich* kept racing through my mind: Quitters never win and winners never quit.

With this thought in mind, I vowed to finish the program. And with the help of Tony and Doris, I kept my promise and graduated at the top of the class.

This story illustrates an important point: You can gain the winner's edge by surrounding yourself with people who support you. You can accomplish anything when you

believe in yourself and take the necessary action to make
your dreams come true.

Quiz 8

1. To gain the winner's edge, you need to _____ _____ in a favorable way.
2. More than ninety percent of your success in learning is due to your belief in your ability to _____.
3. It's much easier to achieve high grades when you like _____.
4. You'll reach the top of the class when you commit to being an excellent _____ and invest your _____ accordingly.
5. To guarantee success, you need to take personal _____ for the results in your classes.
6. To stay motivated, relate each of your classes to your _____ and _____.
7. One of the easiest ways to excel in your classes is to read your _____ early.
8. If you want to have more fun, enroll in classes you _____.
9. One of the best ways to improve your chances for high grades is to get to know your _____.
10. If you want to rise to the top and fly with the eagles, you can't afford to hang around _____.
11. An excellent way to develop belief in yourself is to _____ and _____ successful people.
12. In many cases you can improve your I.Q. and test scores simply by improving your _____.

13. When things don't go your way, the best thing to do is keep a sense of _____.

14. You can accomplish anything when you _____ in yourself and take the necessary _____ to make your dreams come true.

Answers to Quiz 8

1. stand out
2. learn
3. yourself
4. student, time
5. responsibility
6. vision, purpose
7. textbooks
8. enjoy
9. teachers
10. turkeys
11. watch, imitate
12. diet
13. humor
14. believe, action

9

Program Yourself for Success

"You can change who you are by changing what goes into your mind."

In the preceding chapters, you learned one of the easiest and most effective systems ever created for learning and getting top grades. Every feature was outlined step by step.

Still, if you want to guarantee victory, you must prepare your mind in advance. That is, you need to picture yourself as an A student, take a close look at your self-image and program yourself for success.

WHAT IS MY SELF-IMAGE?

Your self-image is the way you see yourself. It's your image of who you are. For example, if you see yourself as an A student, you'll act like an A student. You'll attend your classes, do your homework, study, and get good grades.

Conversely, if you see yourself as a person who hates school, you'll behave that way. You may come to class late, seldom do your homework, study half-heartedly, and get C's, D's and F's.

Either way, you'll act in a manner consistent with how you see yourself.

CAN I CHANGE MY SELF-IMAGE?

Yes.

WHY WOULD I WANT TO?

There is a law of success which states: For things to get better, you've got to get better. For things to change, you've got to change.

Fortunately, you can change who you are by changing what goes into your mind. And since your brain is like a computer, you can either program it for failure . . . or program it for success.

HOW CAN I PROGRAM MYSELF FOR SUCCESS?

First, you need to know that your subconscious mind remembers every detail of your life. It knows every thought, feeling, and mental picture you've ever experienced. Moreover, it never forgets anything and it never sleeps. Your subconscious mind is a lot like Santa Claus: It knows when you are sleeping, it knows when you're awake, it knows when you've been bad and good (so be good for goodness sake!).

Your conscious mind, on the other hand, deals with reason and logic. It's helping you understand this book. Further, it's the part of your mind over which you have complete control. Amazingly, when your conscious mind is relaxed or busily at work on a problem, your subconscious will help you discover ways to get whatever you intensely desire.

For example, have you ever forgot where you left your shoes? You search everywhere for them and you just can't find them. You look under the bed, in the kitchen, in the living room, everywhere! Frustrated, you decide to take a nap. And just as you're about to fall asleep, you suddenly remember you left your shoes in the car.

This is typical of how your subconscious mind works. It helps you find ways to get whatever you repeatedly think about, emotionally dwell upon, and clearly picture in your mind. This is exactly what you were doing when looking for your shoes. And when you relaxed your conscious mind, your subconscious revealed the answer to you.

You also need to know that the "Santa Claus" part of your mind accepts whatever thoughts, feelings, and mental pictures you impress upon it. It doesn't know the difference between good and bad. It simply believes whatever thoughts you choose to think about.

Therefore, if you think of yourself as being stupid, you will believe that you are stupid. Likewise, if you think of yourself as being a top student, you'll believe that you're capable of getting straight A's. In other words, you believe whatever you consistently feed your mind.

Lastly, you need to know that your subconscious mind doesn't know the difference between reality and imagination. You can prove this to yourself by sitting in a comfortable chair and relaxing your mind and body. Close your eyes and imagine the air around you is crisp and clean, like after a morning rain.

See yourself holding a piece of pizza in your hands. Physically use your fingers to hold it. Smell the pepperoni and the mozzarella cheese and feel the warmth of the dough in your palms. Now, take a bite and imagine a string of cheese as it hangs from your mouth to the pizza. Chew slowly and let your tongue taste the crispy bread, the tangy cheese and the spicy pepperoni. Now open your eyes.

If you actively engaged in the preceding exercise, you found you could actually smell and taste the pepperoni pizza.

Your mouth started to water and your stomach began to churn. The reason for this is that your subconscious mind doesn't know the difference between what's real and what's imagined. Moreover, your mind and body respond accordingly. They react the same way regardless of whether you really have an experience or simply create it in your mind.

You believe whatever thoughts, feelings and mental pictures you consistently feed your mind.

You can use this knowledge to program yourself for success and reach your goals. All you need to do is direct your main thoughts, feelings, and mental pictures towards the object of your desire. And then take action!

The following guidelines will help you do just that:

Step 1: Know What You Want

Step 2: Build Your Desire

Step 3: Intensify Your Belief

Step 4: Never Give Up

Step 5: Do What's Necessary

When you follow these steps, your self-image will automatically improve and you'll envision yourself as the person you want to be.

Step 1: Know What You Want

The "Santa Claus" part of your mind is a goal-seeking device. It moves you towards whatever you intensely desire. However, it's up to you to supply it with a target. You must decide exactly what you want and when you want it.

The aim is to keep your thoughts focused on what you want. Perhaps the best way to do this is to record your goal on a piece of paper. Write something similar to the following:

"I am a straight A student. I will receive straight A's on my report card this semester."

Don't worry if these statements are inconsistent with your present self-image. Just scribble them down and imagine yourself as a top student. In doing so, you'll notify your subconscious mind that you're serious about getting high grades.

Step 2: Build Your Desire

Now that you know what you want, you need to get emotionally involved with the benefits of getting top grades. An excellent way to accomplish this is to make a list of your reasons for wanting them. The more reasons you have, the more likely you are to get them.

For instance, you may want to write a statement similar to the following:

"I want straight A's to gain entry into Harvard medical school. I like myself and I'm going to be a family doctor. I want to help thousands of people and I'll receive tremendous rewards for the services I provide my patients."

Write a statement you feel strongly about. You need to be emotionally linked to the words on the page. This announcement will motivate you to take the necessary action to reach your goal.

Even so, you must renew your desire every day. Otherwise your old self-image may pull you down. One of the best ways to keep your spirits up is to surround yourself with things that help you feel good about yourself and your goal. Place these objects where you'll see them throughout your day.

For example, if getting top grades will help you land a "million-dollar" job, you may want to get pictures displaying luxury cars, beautiful homes, exotic yachts, and all the wonderful things your money will buy. Paste these photos on your bathroom mirror, refrigerator, nightstand, notebooks, etc.

Whenever you see them, you'll be reminded of why you're going to school. These thoughts will pump you full of enthusiasm to reach your goal. As a result, you'll start to believe that success is certain to be yours.

1. Recognition from friends, parents and teachers
2. Feeling of accomplishment
3. Scholarship
4. High-paying job
5. A new car from Dad

The more reasons you have for wanting top grades, the more likely you are to get them.

Step 3: Intensify Your Belief

Now that you know what you want and how to build your desire, you must have faith in your ability to succeed. You need to convince yourself you're destined to receive straight A's. Remember, the only way you'll ever succeed is to first believe that you can.

But how can you develop faith? If you're like most people, you've been told things such as, "No! You can't do that! You're stupid! You'll never amount to anything! You're horrible in math! You have a terrible memory!"

You may have heard these statements from parents, teachers, "friends," and (worst of all) yourself. As a result, you may now have a poor self-image in these areas of your life.

Fortunately, you have the power to change your thinking and alter the course of your destiny. Simply tell yourself, "I can do it! I am good in math! I have a great memory!" Keep in mind that your subconscious doesn't know the difference between reality and imagination.

Mix these thoughts with strong emotions and clear mental pictures. But most of all, combine them with positive action. In doing so, you'll change your self-image and become the person you imagine yourself to be.

This type of positive self-talk and positive action is the key to programming yourself for success. The goal is to repeatedly impress your mind with thoughts and images of the person you want to become. But most importantly, imagine yourself as being that person now.

You can accomplish this by writing something like the following on a 3 x 5 index card:

"I am a straight A student. I am receiving straight A's on my report card this semester. I am attending each class, performing all assignments, and studying for all exams. I like myself and I am a great doctor. I am helping thousands of people and receiving tremendous rewards for the services I provide my patients."

Enthusiastically read this statement out loud every evening just before you go to sleep and every morning immediately after rising. As you read, imagine yourself holding a report card overflowing with A's. Make your pictures so real you can't tell the difference between reality and imagination.

Create these images as often as possible throughout your day. As fantastic as it may seem, this simple exercise will intensify your belief and inspire you to become the person you envision yourself to be.

Step 4: Never Give Up

Once you know what you want and believe in your ability to succeed, there's only one way to guarantee success—Never give up. Never, never give up!

When you commit to your goal from beginning to end, you can't fail. You'll always be moving towards a goal that's important to you. Moreover, when you persist until you succeed, there is no such thing as failure. Every setback is a learning experience and every disappointment is an opportunity to learn. As a result, you continue making progress until you finally realize the object of your desire.

An excellent method for developing this habit of persistence is to eliminate the word "try" from your vocabulary. When you say things such as, "I'll try to get straight A's" or "I'll try to be a doctor," you defeat yourself before you start.

These statements tell your subconscious that you'll accept failure. They create images filled with the possibility of defeat. To succeed, you must clean up the thoughts and mental pictures you create in your mind. And you can begin by removing "try" from your stock of words.

Another technique for developing persistence is to list the obstacles that stand between you and your goal. For example, you may want to write something similar to the following:

1. I'll have to sacrifice some leisure time to keep up with my studies.
2. I'll need to take some arithmetic classes to bring my math skills up to speed.
3. I'll have to study subjects I don't enjoy in order to graduate.

This method of listing your roadblocks is very powerful. When you hit one of them, you'll just shrug your shoulders and say, "I knew this was going to happen. I can handle it." Thus, you'll continue pressing forward until you reach your target.

As you probably realize by now, there's only one difference between people who succeed and people who don't. The difference lies in their willingness to continue in spite of all difficulties and set-backs.

If you want to program yourself for success, you must think the same way successful people think. Change your thoughts from "I can't" and "I won't" to "I can" and "I will." Promise yourself you will continue until you succeed—no matter what. This is the only way to guarantee victory.

Nevertheless, there may be times when you feel like giving up. If this should happen, think about your goal and picture the many reasons why getting top grades is important to you. Look at your inspirational photos and fill your mind with renewed passion. Meanwhile, tell yourself "I can do it! I can do it! I can do it!" Program this thought into your subconscious mind.

And remember: Never give up. Never, never give up!

Step 5: Do What's Necessary

No matter who you are, no matter what your background, success requires work. It cannot and will not come to you until you put forth the necessary effort. Moreover, you must exert this energy before you reap the rewards. This is a law of success and it applies to everyone.

Fortunately, if you want to get top grades, simply follow the instructions presented in this book: Program yourself for success, attend your classes, take notes, perform your assignments, study for exams, and master the art of taking tests.

As you've seen, it's easy to carry out each of these steps. Furthermore, you'll gladly perform them as you constantly impress your mind with the many reasons why getting high grades is important to you.

*To get top grades, you must be willing
to do what's necessary.*

THE SUCCESS FORMULA—
A PERSONAL EXPERIENCE

About fourteen years ago I desperately desired
straight A's. At the time, I was planning on being an
airline pilot and was determined to be "The Best!"
I was emotionally crushed, however, when I received
a C on the first philosophy test of the semester.

I'd studied intently for that exam and felt beaten
and worn out. All my dreams seemed to be crum-
bling before my eyes. Nevertheless, I recovered about
a day later and continued to focus on my goal.

My desire for top grades was strong. Still, I
needed to believe in my ability to get them. I told
myself "I can do it! I can do it! I can do it! I'm a
winner! I can get an A in any class!" I repeated these
statements over and over while picturing myself as
an airline pilot surrounded by fifty gorgeous steward-
esses.

I became so inspired I imagined myself attending every class, performing all assignments, and studying for each exam. In addition, I pictured myself holding a report card overflowing with A's. I drilled these thoughts and mental pictures into my mind until I believed I could do it. I believed I could get straight A's!

The thought of being an airline pilot was foremost on my mind throughout the semester. As a result, I devoted quality time to my classes and my scores in philosophy continued to improve during the following weeks. Not only that, I received an A on nearly every test in each of my other classes.

Eventually, the final exam determined my fate in philosophy. I prepared for this test by studying past exams, class notes, and every section of the textbook I'd highlighted throughout the semester. I applied the techniques described in this book and was ready to make my vision of top grades a reality.

The final test was three hours long and I was the last student to finish. The instructor graded the papers and told me I achieved the highest score among all the students in his three classes. As a result, I achieved my goal and received straight A's on my report card.

This story illustrates an important point. You can accomplish your goals, provided you: 1. Know what you want, 2. Build your desire, 3. Intensify your belief, 4. Never give up, and 5. Do what's necessary.

These five steps will improve your self-image and help you get whatever you want. All you need to do is imagine yourself as the person you want to be and take the necessary action to make your dreams come true.

Quiz 9

1. Your _____ is the way you see yourself.
2. When you think _____ thoughts about yourself, you develop a good self-image. When you think _____ thoughts about yourself, you develop a bad self-image.
3. You can change who you are by changing what goes into your _____.
4. Your subconscious mind _____ every detail of your life.
5. Your conscious mind is the part of your mind over which you have complete _____.
6. When your conscious mind is _____ or busily at work on a problem, your subconscious will help you discover ways to get whatever you intensely _____.
7. Your subconscious mind helps you find ways to get whatever you repeatedly _____ about, _____ dwell upon, and clearly _____ in your mind.
8. If you repeatedly envision yourself as an A student, your subconscious mind will help you discover ways to get top _____.
9. You _____ whatever you consistently feed your mind.
10. Your mind and body react the same way regardless of whether you actually have an experience or simply create it in your _____.

11. To program yourself for success, you must direct your main _____, _____, and mental _____ towards the object of your desire.

12. The more _____ you have for wanting top grades, the more likely you are to get them.

13. The only way you'll ever succeed is to first _____ that you can.

14. Positive _____ and positive _____ is the key to programming yourself for success.

15. Once you know what you want and believe in your ability to succeed, there's only one way to guarantee success—Never give _____. Never, never give _____!

16. To guarantee success in any undertaking, you need to: 1. Know what you _____, 2. Build your _____, 3. Intensify your _____, 4. Never give _____ and 5. _____ what's necessary.

Answers to Quiz 9

1. self-image
2. good, bad
3. mind
4. remembers
5. control
6. relaxed, desire
7. think, emotionally, picture
8. grades
9. believe
10. mind
11. thoughts, feelings, pictures
12. reasons
13. believe
14. self-talk, action
15. up, up
16. want, desire, belief, up, Do

10

Put It All Together

*"If you think you can get straight A's, you're right.
If you think you can't get straight A's,
you're still right."*

You now have at your fingertips everything you need to know to get top grades with the least amount of effort. The system is fail-proof and works for all subjects including math, science, history and foreign languages.

You don't have to be a genius. You don't have to "love" school. And you don't have to be the most popular student in class. All you need to do is follow the simple instructions presented in this book.

Fortunately, there are just a few things to keep in mind to guarantee success: Focus on your goals, attend your classes, take notes, perform your assignments, study for exams, and master the art of taking tests.

This chapter will explore these ideas and tie them all together. But most important, it will reveal the secret—the secret of getting straight A's.

WHAT IS THIS SECRET?

It can be summed up in three words: Please your teachers. That's right! That's all you need to do to get outstanding grades.

Get to know your instructors and find out what makes them tick. Determine their likes and dislikes and strive to give them what they want. Make their job as easy and enjoyable as possible. Remember, your teachers are the people you must satisfy to be a top student. By giving them what they want, you'll not only get A's, but learn more in the process.

HOW CAN I MAKE LEARNING EASY?

Keep the following in mind: Anything worth doing is worth doing poorly—until you learn how to do it well. Don't expect to be perfect right away. Attend all your classes and take learning one step at a time.

In doing so, you'll develop a solid foundation on which to build. Moreover, you'll wipe out the fear of failure. Because the more you learn about a subject, the less you fear it and the easier it is to learn.

You can also make learning easy by beginning each school term with an all-out, full-scale attack. Give everything you've got to all your courses the first two or three weeks of class. That is, read your textbooks early and stay current with all assignments.

This habit will inspire you to become more involved and interested in your school work. Furthermore, you'll get a jump on the material and your momentum will often carry you to success.

WHAT IS THE KEY TO CONSTRUCTING VALUABLE NOTES?

It's this: Attend every class, sit in the front row, and document all key ideas mentioned by your teachers. The nine guidelines presented in Chapters 1 and 5 (STLLD WAGA) will help you do just that.

Perfect attendance and taking good notes will do more to improve your grades than anything else.

HOW CAN I GUARANTEE HIGH SCORES ON HOMEWORK?

The trick is to produce work that's pleasing to the eye. Three papers with the exact same content may receive an A, B, or C depending on how they look. Furthermore, if your paper looks good, many instructors will give you an A without even reading all of it.

Even so, you'll need to turn in papers that are on time and accurate as well. You can accomplish this by getting to know your teachers and telling them what they want to hear. For example, if you need to write a term paper, select a topic that interests your teacher and use a word processor to type your work. These computer programs make it easy to check spelling and grammar and make corrections.

Also, have a friend or classmate review your writing. In doing so, you'll surely receive high grades because you're certain to produce neat, accurate, and timely work. Finally, make copies of your homework. While it's unlikely your teacher will lose it, you'll be prepared if they do.

WHAT IS THE KEY TO STUDYING SMART?

Study in short sessions. In other words, bury your head in your books for fifteen to thirty minutes. Then, take a "five-minute" break before going back to work. These recesses will give you a chance to relax, sort and store the information. As a result, you'll remember more in less time.

The reason for this is that it's easier to recall the details covered at the beginning and end of a study session. These are the times when your concentration is at its peak. On the other hand, the material covered during the middle of a session is often "forgotten." This middle-time is when your concentration is at its lowest.

You can prove this to yourself by reciting the following words to a friend: enchilada, inoperative, misinterpret, repercussion, continuation, sensibility and unscramble. Do not mention how many items are in the list. Just recite each one and ask your friend to repeat the first . . . the last . . . and then the middle word.

Chances are, your companion will easily recall the first and last words. However, the middle ones will be very difficult to recall.

You can use this knowledge to reduce the time you spend studying. Simply study for a reasonable amount of time (fifteen to thirty minutes), take a short break, and repeat this process over and over. By doing this, you'll increase the number of sessions every time you sit down to work. Thus, you'll increase the amount of information you can easily recall.

As a final note, avoid studying for more than two hours at a time. Give yourself a chance to grasp the information. For instance, if you need to study for four hours, take a long break (twenty to thirty minutes) half way through. Listen to some soothing music, relax in your favorite chair, or take a nap.

These long quiet breaks will allow the information to set in your brain. When you go back to studying, you'll have more energy and renewed concentration.

HOW CAN I MOTIVATE MYSELF TO STUDY?

The key is to link more pleasure than pain with studying. You can accomplish this by thinking of the benefits rather than the pitfalls of completing your tasks.

For instance, what do average students focus on when they think about homework? Typically, they envision all the pain and suffering commonly associated with it: Long hours in the library, tedious reading assignments, etc. As a result, they lack drive and energy because they create unhappy pictures in their minds.

On the other hand, what do you concentrate on when you think about studying? Chances are, you focus on the rewards: better grades, scholarships, high-paying jobs, and increased knowledge. In addition, you may even carry a photograph that reminds you of why you're going to school. When you look at this image, you create a state of mind that inspires you to forge ahead.

Amazingly, you'll be motivated even more as you continue to get your body physically involved. You've probably experienced the following many times throughout your life: It's Saturday morning and you need to clean your bedroom. Nevertheless, all you can think about is the pain and drudgery of dusting, vacuuming and cleaning.

Still, you force yourself to grab a dust rag and start to clean your room.

Suddenly, for no clear reason, you're filled with energy. You polish the furniture, wash the walls, clean the windows, vacuum under the bed, sweep out the closet, wash down the light fixtures, and neaten your dresser drawers. The simple act of dusting your room inspired you to launch a full-scale attack.

You can use this insight to motivate yourself to study. Typically, all you need to do is sit at a desk, open your book, and start to perform your first assignment. Meanwhile, focus your attention on the many reasons why getting high grades is important to you.

This simple exercise will inspire you to continue pressing forward until all your work is done. As a result, you'll complete your assignments right away. Not only that, you'll eliminate the pain you might otherwise experience if you were to come to class unprepared.

HOW CAN I DEVELOP A SUPER MEMORY?

You can become a memory expert by forcing yourself to think of information in a variety of ways. In other words, examine carefully the material you want to recall. Then think of it in unusual and creative ways. That way, you'll involve more of your senses in the learning process.

For example, suppose you want to commit to memory the ten study tips presented in Chapter 3:

1. Make a List
2. Choose a Primary Study Spot
3. Set Aside Enough Time
4. Study by Yourself
5. Keep Your Desk Free from Clutter
6. Take Frequent Breaks
7. Avoid Eating
8. Spend Your Reading Time Wisely

9. Use School to Make Your Life Easier

10. Focus on Rewards

You can force yourself to remember this list by selecting one key word from each study tip. In this case you may want to choose the following:

List

Primary

Time

Yourself

Clutter

Breaks

Eating

Reading

Easier

Rewards

Next, write the first letter of each key word on a piece of paper: L P T Y C B E R E R. Then, use your imagination to form a sentence using words that begin with these letters.

For instance, you can rearrange the letters (T L R R C B Y P E E) to create: The Little Red Rider Can Be Your Pal Every Easter.

With a little practice, you'll associate the T with Time, the L with List, the first R with Reading, the second R with Rewards, the C with Clutter, the B with Breaks, the Y with Yourself, the P with Primary, the first E with Eating and the final E with Easier.

These key words will cause you to remember the ten study tips. Moreover, once you've thought of them, you'll recall at least one paragraph of information about each.

At this point, you may be wondering whether you'll be able to recall the unusual sentence you just created. If so, close your eyes and picture yourself studying during recess with the little red rider. He's three feet tall and wearing a bright red coat. Suddenly, a gigantic teacher walks up to you and says, "The Little Red Rider Can Be Your Pal Every Easter." In a short time, you'll be able to recall this ridiculous sentence whenever you need to list the ten study tips. And like a chain reaction, you'll remember the ten key words and all the information associated with them.

As you can see, it's easy to develop a super memory when you examine carefully what you want to recall and force yourself to think of the information in unusual and creative ways. In doing so, you'll involve many of your senses in the learning process. And since there's a direct relationship between your senses and your memory, you'll easily recall the information whenever you desire.

WHAT IS THE KEY TO PREPARING FOR EXAMS?

The secret is this: Anticipate the test questions and commit your answers to memory. That is, review your class notes, homework problems, reading assignments, and past exams. Then, make up questions you feel will be on your upcoming test and file the answers in your mind. Finally, give yourself a practice exam using the questions you just created.

Write your answers on a piece of paper while reciting the information out loud. This exercise will dramatically increase your recall and boost your confidence on the day of the test. After all, you'll probably have studied the answers to most of the questions you'll find on the actual exam.

HOW CAN I GUARANTEE HIGH GRADES ON TESTS?

Once you've anticipated the test questions and committed the answers to memory, it's easy to achieve high grades on tests. All you need to do is tell your teachers what they want to hear and make their job as easy as possible.

For example, if you're taking an essay exam, include a lot of details in your answers. Volume is important. In addition, make your paper easy to read by using short words, short paragraphs, and appropriate headings. By doing this, you're likely to receive a top score.

Remember, three test papers with the exact same content may receive an A, B, or C, depending on how they look. And as stated earlier, if your paper looks real sharp some teachers will give you an A without even reading all of it.

Three papers with the exact same content may receive an A, B or C depending on how they look.

As a final note, you can encourage instructors to give you high marks by asking them to telephone you with your test results. Or perhaps you can leave a self-addressed postcard requesting your final score. This approach, combined with your neat, accurate test papers, is certain to produce top grades.

WHAT CAN I DO TO GUARANTEE SUCCESS (IN SCHOOL AND IN LIFE)?

To be sure of victory in any undertaking, remember this: The biggest obstacle standing between you and success is the way that you think. If you think you can get straight A's, you're right. If you think you can't get straight A's, you're still right.

Your thoughts are like magnets that attract what you think about. If you want to reach your goals, you need to keep your thoughts focused on what you want and off what you don't want. Read the preceding sentence again. It's the secret to your success (and the key to being happy). Learn it and you'll succeed. Ignore it and you won't.

For example, you've probably found yourself saying such things as, "I knew I was going to miss that shot" or "I knew I was going to screw up." These thoughts almost guarantee a missed shot or a screw-up.

On the other hand, you've probably imagined yourself succeeding by thinking such things as, "I knew I was going to make that shot" or "I knew I was going to win that game." As a result, it's likely you made the shot and/or won the game.

The point is this: You need to control the focus of your thoughts. Because whatever you focus on is what you'll get. The following steps will help you put this idea into action and achieve every goal you set for yourself:

Know What You Want

Build Your Desire

Intensify Your Belief

Never Give Up

Do What's Necessary

Follow these instructions and you're certain to win. When you commit to your goal from beginning to end, you can't fail. You'll simply be working towards something that's important to you. Moreover, when you persist until you succeed, there is no such thing as failure. Every set-back is a learning experience and every disappointment is an opportunity to learn. As a result, you continue making progress until you finally realize the object of your desire.

IS THERE ANYTHING ELSE I NEED TO KNOW ABOUT GETTING TOP GRADES?

No. Everything has already been presented. The system is fail-proof and works for all subjects. However, the only way to know that it works is to use it for yourself. Only then will you experience the results. Only then will you realize how easy it is to study, learn and get, straight A's!

Quiz 10

1. The secret of getting straight A's is: Please your _____.

2. The more you _____ about a subject, the less you fear it and the easier it is to _____.

3. You can make learning easy by beginning each school term with an all-out, full-scale _____.

4. The key to constructing valuable notes is this: _____ every class, sit in the _____ row, and document all _____ ideas mentioned by your teachers.

5. Three homework papers with the exact same content may receive an A, B, or C, depending on how they _____.

6. To guarantee high grades on homework, you need to produce _____, _____, _____ work.

7. The key to studying smart is this: Study in _____ sessions.

8. It's easiest to remember the information covered at the _____ and _____ of a study session.

9. To motivate yourself to study, focus on the _____ and take immediate _____.

10. It's easy to develop a super memory when you carefully examine the information you want to recall and force yourself to think of it in _____ and _____ ways.

11. The key to preparing for exams is this: Anticipate the _____ questions and commit your answers to _____.

12. Three test papers with the exact same content may receive an A, B, or C, depending on how they _____.

13. To guarantee high test scores, you need to produce _____, _____ papers filled with lots of _____.

14. Whenever you're given a writing assignment, you can make your papers easier to read by using _____ words, _____ paragraphs, and appropriate _____.

15. To program yourself for success, keep your thoughts focused on what you _____ and off what you don't _____.

16. The success formula is: 1. Know what you _____, 2. Build your _____, 3. Intensify your _____, 4. Never give _____ and 5. _____ what's necessary.

17. You need to control the focus of your _____. Because whatever you focus on is what you'll _____.

18. When you commit to your goal from _____ to _____, you can't fail.

19. The biggest obstacle standing between you and success is the way that you _____.

20. If you _____ you can get straight A's, you're right. If you _____ you can't get straight A's, you're still right.

Answers to Quiz 10

1. teachers
2. learn, learn
3. attack
4. attend, front, key
5. look
6. neat, accurate, timely
7. short
8. beginning, end
9. rewards, action
10. unusual, creative
11. test, memory
12. look
13. neat, accurate, details
14. short, short, headings
15. want, want
16. want, desire, belief, up, Do
17. thoughts, get
18. beginning, end
19. think
20. think, think

Afterword

I wrote this book out of a sincere desire to help you learn more in less time with higher retention. I wanted to take the mystery out of going to school, learning, and getting good grades. But most of all, I wanted to make your life easier by giving you a proven roadmap for success.

Although I've never done very well on intelligence tests, I developed most of this system for getting good grades when I was eight years old. I have personally used it to maintain an A average throughout grade school, junior high, high school, college, and graduate school. Clearly, the techniques work.

Of course, change is a never-ending process. And as my knowledge expands, this book will be updated appropriately. I'd be delighted to hear from you for future editions. Feel free to share your successes and indicate what chapters were particularly helpful. Offer your suggestions for improvement and let me know what still puzzles you.

As a final thought, I'd like to say that it's been a sincere pleasure writing this book and I hope it proves of value to you. I feel I know you and I hope that one day we shall meet. Until then, best wishes and best of luck!

Sincerely,

Brian Marshall

Recommended Listening

Canfield, Jack. *How To Build High Self-Esteem: A Practical Process for Personal Growth.* Chicago:
  Nightingale-Conant Corp., 1989.

Dawson, Roger. *Secrets of Power Performance.*
  Chicago: Nightingale-Conant Corp., 1990.

Dyer, Wayne. *How To Be a No-Limit Person.*
  Chicago: Nightingale-Conant Corp., 1987.

Hill, Napolean. *Think and Grow Rich.*
  Palm Desert, CA: Guthy-Renker Corp., 1988.

Robbins, Anthony. *Unlimited Power.*
  Chicago: Nightingale-Conant Corp., 1986.

Stone, W. Clement, and Napolean Hill. *Success Through a Positive Mental Attitude.*
  Chicago: Nightingale-Conant Corp., 1987.

Tracy, Brian. *The Psychology of Success: Ten Proven Principles for Winning.*
  Chicago: Nightingale-Conant Corp., 1986.

Waitley, Denis. *The Psychology of Winning*.
    Chicago: Nightingale-Conant Corp., 1987.

Waitley, Denis, and Thomas Budzynski. *The Subliminal Winner*.
    Chicago: Nightingale-Conant Corp., 1987.

Ziglar, Zig. *Success and the Self-Image: Inspiring Greatness in Yourself*.
    Carrollton, TX: Zig Ziglar Corp., 1988.

To find out more about the above programs, check your local public library or write to:

Nightingale-Conant Corporation
7300 Lehigh Avenue
Chicago, Illinois 60648

Index

161

My Notes

Give the Secret of Getting Straight A's to Your Friends and Fellow Students!

ORDER FORM

YES, I want _____ copies of *The Secret of Getting Straight A's* at $12.95 each, plus $3 shipping per book. (California residents please include $1.00 state sales tax.) Canadian orders must be accompanied by a postal money order in U.S. funds. Allow 30 days for delivery.

_____ Check/money order enclosed

Name _____ Phone _____

Address _____

City _____

State/Zip _____

Please make your check payable and return to:

Hathaway International Publications
P.O. Box 6543
Buena Park, CA 90622-6543